AUTHOR S NOTE.

Fair warning, the topics covered in this book are basic and more likely to help those just starting out on their publishing journey, rather than experienced authors.

Other titles by
Danielle Ackley-McPhail

THE ETERNAL CYCLE SERIES
Yesterday's Dreams
Tomorrow's Memories
Today's Promise

THE ETERNAL WANDERINGS SERIES
Eternal Wanderings

THE BAD-ASS FAERIE TALE SERIES
The Halfling's Court
The Redcap's Queen
The High King's Fool
(forthcoming)

Baba Ali and the Clockwork Djinn
(with Day Al-Mohamed)

The Literary Handyman
Build-A-Book Workshop

The Ginger KICK! Cookbook

SHORT FICTION
A Legacy of Stars
Transcendence
Consigned to the Sea
Flash in the Can
The Die Is Cast
(with Mike McPhail)

The Literary Handyman
More Tips
From the Handyman

Danielle Ackley-McPhail

PAPER
PHOENIX

PRESS

Pennsville, NJ

PUBLISHED BY
Paper Phoenix Press
A division of eSpec Books
PO Box 242
Pennsville, NJ 08070
www.especbooks.com

Copyright © 2021 Danielle Ackley-McPhail

ISBN: 978-1-949691-65-8
ISBN (ebook): 978-1-949691-64-1

Interior Design: Danielle McPhail
www.sidhenadaire.com

Literary Handyman Icon: Bryan Prindiville
Cover Design: Mike McPhail

Copyediting: Greg Schauer

Dedication

To those with the courage not only to spill your hearts
onto the page, but to show it to the world.

Contents

Honing Your Craft

Getting Down to Business

A Quick Note from the Handyman

Hello, and welcome! Or, should I say, my condolences… ?

Two points before I begin—three, if you need informing that I'm not actually a handy*man*, but then, I think for most of you, the cover will have given that away.

Point one: This series is and always has been a helping hand to those just beginning their exploration of writing and publishing. It will cover topics established authors will likely consider very basic. I tell you this upfront so that you are not disappointed with this book for being exactly what it was intended to be.

Point two: This is not an instructional guide. These are tips I share with you from the far side of nearly thirty years' experience working in publishing and nearly twenty years' experience as a published author. I am not a teacher, and this is not a textbook. It is my hope that the topics I do cover here will help you polish your craft and gain insight into the world of publishing without having to go through all the intervening years that I did. Because these are articles that have been written across a period of years, there will be some repetition, but each article does cover a separate—if at times related—topic. I come from a speculative fiction background, but most of what I have written here will apply to any genre.

This venture you are about to embark on will be filled with joy and wonder, but with an equal—or disproportionate amount of frustration, as the case may be. Really, it depends on your luck. Not saying that to discourage you, just to brace you for the hard, realistic facts. Aspiring to be an author is not an easy dream, but it can be a fulfilling one.

I will share with you the advice I gave in the first *Literary Handyman* book: consider this a dedicated hobby, that way, when success hits, you are pleasantly surprised, and if that takes a while, you are not bitterly disappointed.

As with most things in life, success is not solely based on skill and hard work but also on luck and opportunity. But remember, if you give up, you have guaranteed failure.

On that cheery note… shall we begin?

Dream Big!

Danielle Ackley-McPhail

Honing Your Craft

The Author's Opening Salvo: Book Titles

You know, there are a hell of a lot of books out there.

(Yeah, I know... *Duh!*)

So, sarcasm aside, how do we keep them all straight? There is so much information associated with a book: the author's name, the publisher, the ISBN, but first and foremost is the title. In most cases, that is the first and maybe only bit of information your audience is going to know.

Guess it better be good, right?

This article was inspired by comments I received on an article from *The Literary Handyman*, "The Naming of Names," where I go in-depth on naming characters. Well, books are a writer's children just as much as any born from their loins — or imagination — and should garner a similar level of thought in naming, so let's get down to it, shall we?

Getting it Right

You know, some parents will be outraged at this next comment, but I dare say it is more critical to get the name of your book right than it is those of your children. Why? Well... a child might hate their name, but there is always the option of a nickname, or should you truly cock it up, legal name changes. Basically, your children have options. Your books, not so much... Once you release a book, it is very unlikely any significant change will ever be made in the title (unlikely, not impossible, before you protest, but I'll get to that later.) Why do I assume that the title is the first — and possibly only — aspect of your book your audience will encounter? Well, if you should be fortunate enough to have your book shelved on a physical bookstore shelf, the majority of books are spine out. If you don't make it into a brick-and-mortar store, you have to consider that many internet or database searches do not always display with images, or when book sites do return images, they are often of a size that doesn't really do justice to the cover. That makes a good title even more vital. Because of this, the name of your book must stand and represent. Here are some points you need to consider when thinking about potential titles:

- *Is it catchy?* The best corollary to a book title is a jingle from a commercial. Short, sweet, and clever ones tend to linger in a person's memory. Because of this, many (but not all) titles tend to be four or less words (counting articles), and they tend to "pop" as they say in the industry, for example: White Trash Zombie, Bad-Ass Faeries, A Series of Unfortunate Events (Lemony Snicket). All of those are attention-getters or have some sort of shock value that imprints them on people's brains.

- *Is it easy to remember?* Titles shouldn't be too complicated or long because those aspects increase the potential for a person to either forget them or remember them incorrectly. Because many of us depend on word-of-mouth to expand our audiences, it is vital to facilitate those talking about a book getting the title correct.

- *Is it relevant?* What does the title say about the book? You have to think about the title as your one-floor elevator pitch. It needs to catch your audience's attention, catch it quickly, and hold it. If the title doesn't intrigue the audience, you have lost your first, best opportunity to inspire them to consider the book further. You want them curious enough to pick it up and read the back, or in the case of the internet, click on the link to read further. To that end, the title should reflect something of the tone and subject matter of the book. It doesn't have to be overt... sometimes subtle works really well in making a book intriguing... however, there can be an extremely fine line between intriguing and confusing. (Make sure you know which side of the line you're on.)

- *Is it distinct?* As I mentioned, there are many different identifiers for a book that should make it simple for a reader to be sure they have the one they are after — preferably yours. However, you can't assume your audience will have all those details when trying to find your book. After all, we depend on human memory here, in many cases, or idle references made on internet blogs or such, where those making the post may not see a need to be thorough with including certain details.

What's In A Title?

So... I know what you're saying now. How the heck does that help me come up with titles? Fair enough. Believe me, these points are relevant once you have a few ideas on the table, so to speak. Just keep them in the back of your mind while I go into some of the approaches you can take to the task.

Theme – Determine the theme of your work and try to incorporate that into a title. For my first novel, *Yesterday's Dreams*, sacrifice and self-discovery were two overriding themes for the book. The title referred to a key location in the book, a pawnshop, but it also referred to the sacrifices the main character makes for her family as she gives up first a career as a concert violinist and then her prized violin. That is the first relevance. It also refers to the character coming into her own when she feared there was nothing left for her. So dreams let go and dreams achieved.

Another example from my work is the series *Bad-Ass Faeries*. This meets all of the above bullet points quite handily, but in relation to the theme, we started the series to bring the popular perception of faeries back to the roots of the legends where the fae were malevolent, mischievous, or warriors... not cute and fluffy. When you read the title, you know you aren't going to be reading about <insert major franchise here> faerie princesses... unless they are also warriors.

Genre – which one are you writing in? This is relevant for two reasons. One: if you are writing genre, you are generally writing to a very narrow target audience and there are often certain conventions in titles you might want to take into account. Doesn't mean you have to follow them, but you should be aware. Two: genre writing has distinct characteristics that the title should reflect so the potential reader is more likely to recognize that your work is what they are looking for. My example for this is *In An Iron Cage: The Magic of Steampunk,* an anthology I once edited. This one we have to pick apart a bit. The "In An Iron Cage" part is catchy and intriguing but doesn't really tell you what the collection is about. The subtitle "The Magic of Steampunk" clarifies this is a steampunk anthology and that the stories include magical elements, which identifies the book as both steampunk and fantasy.

Tone – Is your story or book serious or humorous? Is it full of drama or romance? It seems obvious enough, but this is very important to sort out. After all, you don't want a joke title on a serious book because the audience will expect the title to reflect what they are going to read. For example: *The Hitchhiker's Guide to the Galaxy* by Douglass Adams. With a title like that, you expect the contents of the book to be humorous. By contrast, *The Amityville Horror* by Jay Anson (yeah... I had to look it up too...) tells you right up front that the story is frightening.

Concept – is there some defining idea in the book that would be interesting to the reader that you can allude to in the title? I'm working on a science fiction story at the moment that involves theoretical travel beyond known space. In doing my research, I ran into a bit of information in a Dark Matter article about a reference ancient mapmakers use to place on their maps for unknown areas: Terra Incognita. That was a fun fact, and given the concept of my story and the fact that it had to deal with space travel, I had to name the story *Astra Incognita*. Not everyone will get the historical reference I'm alluding to, but they will—I hope—be intrigued enough to read on! And hey, for those who do get the reference, they will be thrilled and feel like they are in on a secret, and again—I hope—eager to see where I'm going with it.

Play on Words – I develop a lot of anthologies from concept to completion. I often start with just an idea or a title, or sometimes a piece of art that inspires a title. One of those collections is *Dragon's Lure*. See, I have a couple of books to my credit with dragons on the cover, but no dragons in the stories (don't ask), much to the disappointment of dragon fans. That made me realize I had a market for a dragon book if I could come up with an idea. For something different, I figured it would be good to explore the concept of why world mythology attributes certain things as lures for dragons… like virgins and the moon or nests of gems. So the book is both about dragon lore and dragon lures, thus the title. Now, like I said, I started out with the title in that case, so it's kind of a cheat as an example, but you get what I mean, right?

Now I am sure that there are other things you could consider, but rather than go on and on, it's time to cover some other relevant points.

The Business Side of Titles

Working titles. A lot of writers have what they call a working title in the beginning. It's not really what they want for a final name, but it gives them something to reference when talking about it and something to name the file on their computer. It's kind of like calling a baby or a pet "sweetie" or something cute like that until you get around to no longer bickering over what to call them. (unfortunately… my cat, Baby, got stuck with his pre-name). Of course, you might decide that you're comfortable with your working title by the time you are done… or conversely, your publisher, in the end, may consider your *final title* the working title and proceed to tell you what it's actually going to be.

Will the Real Book Title Please Stand Up

Names repeat, whether they are for children, characters, or books. It just happens, hard to avoid with the combined volume of all three in the world. Of course, with books, you have a hope of minimizing any overlap. Nothing says two books can't have the same title, but you want to be cautious and think through the ramifications. Do some research and see if there are other books out there with the same title. If it is an older title, I wouldn't be too concerned, the way I would if it was a recent release. I definitely would think twice if the other book (or books) are in the same genre or have the same topic as yours because that is just asking for confusion among the reading audience... like I said, sometimes all they have is a title to go on so if you have two books with the same title and different authors, there is only a 50-50 chance they'll pick the right one if they are after yours. The odds get exponentially worse if there is more than one already out there. I have a friend, L. Jagi Lamplighter, who ran into this problem. Her manuscript—which she had been working on for something like ten years—was titled Prospero's Daughter. Somewhere in the middle of her working on the manuscript, someone else released a book with her title. Both are fantasies. My friend eventually sold and released her book, and while the publisher wasn't too concerned about the title issue, my friend was uncomfortable with it and changed the name to *Prospero Lost*. Two more sequels have since released in this series... which brings me to my next topic.

Series Titles

Like subtitles, series titles help tell a bit more about books that are linked, if nothing else, identifying that they go together. In the case of Ms. Lamplighter's books, her original title, *Prospero's Daughter*, became her series title, thus allowing her to retain the title she liked and providing more information on the series, which are all from Miranda's perspective (the books are based on the characters from Shakespeare's *Tempest*).

I have several series that I am associated with in one capacity or another, and the fact that there is a series title lets the reader know there are more books out there. For instance, *Yesterday's Dreams* is book one in the *Eternal Cycle* series (followed by *Tomorrow's Memories* and *Today's Promise*). I have another novel, *The Halfling's Court: A Bad-Ass Faerie Tale*. In this instance, the subtitle is also the series title, as subsequent books in the series will have the same subtitle. In addition to identifying them as a part of a series, it also links the books to their origins, the *Bad-Ass Faeries* anthologies.

Basically, creating a series is creating a brand. All the above applies, only it has relevance for all the books under that series title, so some forethought needs to go into the process. Of course, sometimes you don't realize you are writing a series until after the fact, sometimes after the first book is already published. That's when you roll with it and hope the publisher is willing to submit a corrected cover after the fact; otherwise, your only recourse (short of getting a new publisher) is to link the books as a series on the internet so that a search of the first book turns up information on the subsequent books.

Summing Up

I could say more, but I am afraid it would be difficult to cover everything in a reasonable space and time (besides… my lunch hour is over), so I'll end it here and leave something to talk about another time…

This article was a little hard for me to write. Coming up with titles is fairly easy for me. I discovered that *explaining* how to come up with titles is not. There are so many aspects that go into naming a book or story, and it is such a personal process. I hope this advice gave you something to think about and at least a direction to forge in to allow you to sort this out for yourself. There is no one right way, after all.

Keeping It Short – When the Words Count

In writing, as in everything else, most of us have a natural range. Some people are right-handed, some people left, and just to screw up the curve, some can use either hand interchangeably. You have sopranos... tenors... basses, and the rare vocalist who can manage to bounce all along the range. In writing, it is a touch simpler.

Some people excel at novels, others at short fiction. (We don't talk about those who can do either one with ease... they tend to get a lot of dirty looks from other writers.) Now, just because you have an innate length doesn't mean you can't hone your ability to write longer or shorter. It's all about scope and scale. If you can get a handle on those, you can run up and down the word-count range with the best of them, no matter your natural impulses.

Think of a short story as what you see through a telephoto lens. You zoom in right on a narrow image and capture it. You go for the crisp, tight detail, and it's all about that. Short stories capture an instant, a single thread. There are generally only a few characters dealing with one event or goal. The action/tension comes fast, and every word leads toward the resolution, with little to no wandering. It is more about what is happening than who it is happening to. Don't get me wrong... this doesn't mean you get a free pass on characterization. What it does mean is that in short fiction, character details tend to be the type that move the plot forward, whereas, in longer works, the author has more room to explore the character's depths for their own sake and not for what they offer toward resolving the plot.

Now, nothing is universal. There are always exceptions, but for the purpose of discussion, I have outlined some of the usual differences between short fiction and novels. Just know… if there is a "rule" somewhere, writers will break it…

Short Story	Novel
• Detail relevant to the plot	• Detail relevant to the plot
	• Detail that builds the characters and universe
• Brief build-up with limited action/tension leading to the resolution	• Detailed build-up with multiple actions/tension leading to the resolution
• Single thread of action	• Multiple action threads
• Single character Point of View	• One or more character Points of View
	• Secondary, tertiary, and background characters
• Scale is equivalent to a scene or an episode	• Scale is equivalent to a movie or series season.

Establishing Character in Short Fiction

Short stories have a limit. Go past that limit, and they are no longer short stories. This is a fundamental fact many writers have trouble grasping (says the editor who has received 15,000-word "short" stories). So, how do you keep the words reined in and still have a distinct, recognizable character? You cherry-pick details. Find one or two elements that make your character unique and introduce them early, then find ways to reinforce those elements throughout the story without going into great detail. For example, I have a character named Scotch. He's a wiseass. Most of the time, this does not come into play, but once in a while, a natural progression in the dialogue will leave an opening for a smart-ass comment. Scotch never misses an opportunity to jump in. It is always brief and always about what is already happening, but it is enough to set this character off from Kat, his sarcastic, "straight-man" companion. Now for Kat, I use two things to distinguish her... at random times, the events happening inspire thoughts of her PawPaw that somehow tie into what is happening, and when she is tense, her gun is like her security blanket. Those aren't a lot to go on when defining who a person is, but they are distinct enough details that you feel you know them and care what happens to them when I keep dealing them blow after blow on the way to the climactic ending.

Keep Your Eye on the Goal

As a short story writer, you have one goal: Keep it short. That means your characters have one goal. Stick to that one goal, and you can write a short story. Start pulling in multiple threads and get ready to find beta readers for another novel. In a short story, everything that happens should have the express purpose of taking you one step closer to the story's resolution. Anything that doesn't do that has to go. Okay... most of everything that doesn't do that has to go. (Like I said... writers... rules... things are going to break.)

Doing a 180

Not going to spend too much time on this, but I wanted to at least touch on it, because, you know, some people have the opposite problem. How do you move past short to novel-length? It helps if you think of a novel as a series of short stories all headed in the same direction, only not in an orderly fashion. They jumble together, touch, and even trample across each other's paths until threads get tangled, but in the end... if you do your job right... it all makes satisfying sense. The difference in a novel is that some of these "stories" are the getting-to-know-you kind, while others are the action-packed rush. The key is that each one builds on the next, with all the little sub-threads coming together for an overall goal.

Summing Up

So... have short stories frustrated you in the past? Feel there is always more story to tell until suddenly you have a book? If you want to keep it short, keep it tight. Ease your way in. Maybe try writing one encapsulated scene. Pick a character. Pick one goal. Pick one conflict. Pick one opponent. Find a twist. Find a solution. Do that over and over. Make it complete. Don't worry about if it is a full story. Just get used to dealing with one goal. Make it interesting, make it intense, either with action or emotion. When you are done, take a look and see what things look like under a microscope. It doesn't matter if there is more story to tell as long as you resolved your scene's primary objective. After all, nothing says you can't just write another story!

Serial Tendencies –
Why Some Writers Are More Than A Little Mad

(Originally published in The Writer's Toolbox, Allegory Magazine.)

Well, as you might have noticed… the world did, in fact, not end.

Hard to believe, I know, but there it is. That makes this now "The Rest of Your Life, Part II." Rather appropriate as I'm in the mood to talk about the insanity of series writing.

Even if you haven't finished writing your first book, don't start thinking this article will be of no use to you. Not only might you be taken with the feverish desire to write a series someday, but in the here-and-now, a lot of what I'm going to recommend may come in handy with a stand-alone novel as well, or for those of you who write serial short fiction.

So… you. Sit back down and start reading!

A Matter of Focus

This is the difference, really. Writing is writing, but the scale determines the type of focus a writer needs to have. To give you an idea of what I'm talking about, I will give you a brief outlook on each of the different types of fiction writing first, as they relate to focus. (Keep in mind, nothing is absolute. These are just what are most common. The focus terms are mine just for the purpose of this article, not something established.)

MicroFiction: Pinpoint focus – These stories are called many other things, but this is the name I use. It is a story that is somewhere between 1 and 99 words, an insane number. A brief interaction where economy of words forces the reader to infer the greater story represented. Think sound bite.

Flash: Tight focus – A story between 100 and 1500 words. One scene generally, with little attention paid to the background or characters beyond the literary equivalent of an establishing shot. The story deals with one point in time and one goal. Think commercial.

Short: Individual focus – A story between 1500 and 10,000 words. To simplify, think of these as A-Day-In-The-Life type stories. That doesn't mean it literally is only one day, but the plot generally deals with one character or group in a specific situation. One storyline. Think television episode.

Novel: Communal focus – A story between 10,000 and beyond, including Novelettes and Novellas. More intricate than all the others mentioned, this deals with the broader environment for a character, group of characters, or community. There is generally a primary plot and several related subplots woven together to reach a central goal. The setting and community are more developed, as is the back story, but generally in the context of the plot, with collateral details there but less developed. Think miniseries.

Series/Shared Universe: World focus – A collection of linked short stories or novels against a common backdrop, written by the same author, or by various authors following the same world bible. Sometimes with an ongoing overall storyline, sometimes not. Not only are there multiple plotlines, a whole cast of characters, and the greater backdrop of community, world, and even universe, but there is a depth of detail that turns the backdrop into a major character in its own right. The writer needs to know how things interact or could interact if a given situation were to occur, even if it never does. This is an intricate tapestry of characters, settings, and events. Think long-running series.

The Insanity of Series Writing

It's hard enough to write a novel, right? Making sure your primary characters are well-developed, that the setting is established and makes sense, and that subplots and the primary plot are resolved by the last page. Depending on how complex your novel is, that can be a lot of detail to keep straight. Imagine doing that for a series, where continuity needs to be maintained from book to book, and the primary plotline is not generally resolved until the very end… whenever that might be.

Pulling a series off well takes coordination. Now, I'm not just talking things like outlines and synopses, particularly as not everyone works well with those. But there are several other tricks you can use to keep things in order.

Character Sheets - You can get elaborate and create an actual sheet, like gamers use, or you can just keep note cards (physical or virtual) on each character. There are also writing programs—like Scrivener—that have a built-in system for tracking your characters. Whatever method you choose, here is some of the basic information you should track and update as needed: hair, eyes, build, scars, distinguishing features/behaviors, relationships, habits, skills, experience. Not only does this information help you to depict the character accurately as you write the series, but it also helps you to understand who they are. You want to include deeper background on primary characters even if the information doesn't appear in the book(s) because this is the type of information that affects your characters' decisions when confronted with a situation. Additionally, it can help you track how they have become who they are through the progression of the series. This can be important if you find that they are coming off the wrong way or too one-note.

Timeline - These can get real complicated, depending on your story and how many characters you have. They not only help to keep track of when things happen, but who they happen to and how that affects other events elsewhere in the story. By maintaining timelines, you can weave things more tightly together. If you have a very complex series, you will want to consider several different timelines. One for each primary or even secondary character, and a combined timeline of everything that happens. Not only does this help you keep things straight, but it also is a tool you can use if you need to backtrack and add an unplanned scene. The timeline will give you a better understanding of where that information needs to go depending on what has to happen before and after and which characters you need to involve in the scene.

Story Board - Even if you don't outline, chances are you have some idea of the major points you have to hit to get where you are going. Using sketches or note cards, you can create a visual timeline that is easy to rearrange as needed. It gives you flexibility and also helps you to see where you need to fill in gaps. You can also track individual story arcs by color coding or marking in some other distinct way so that you can keep things straight no matter how complex.

Focus - This differs from the focus mentioned above. This focus is about keeping your eye on the goal, to digress into cliché. When writing a series — primarily the -logy (duology, trilogy, etc.) — you have to always keep in mind where you want/need to end up. This is often complicated because it can be a long time between the first and subsequent novels. It's sometimes easy to forget where you are going when the journey can take years to complete. Beyond that, each individual book must have a focus of its own, a subplot that will make it a satisfying read in and of itself beyond the overall story arc. This is important because (1) you want to end up where you're supposed to, and (2) you don't want the series to have too many unrelated tangents to confuse matters. See, when you start to develop something that ends up going nowhere, it can really piss off the fans.

Why We Do It

Why would we, as writers, invite such a headache? Why would we live years with so many personalities crammed into our brains waiting to come out? There are several reasons for this.

First, sometimes a story is just too big to tell in one book. That happened with my Eternal Cycle trilogy—*Yesterday's Dreams, Tomorrow's Memories*, and *Today's Promise*. The story started out as a young girl sacrificing her heirloom—an enchanted violin—to save her family's home. She discovers she is something more than human, can do magic, and that both the good and evil figures of mythology are real beings who want to either protect or use her. In my research, I discovered a myth of Carman and her three sons. They terrorized ancient Ireland until they were destroyed by the Sidhe (Celtic Elves). As the Sidhe were my good magical creatures, Carman and her sons were the perfect counterpoints. Unfortunately, trying to deal with all those characters at once would have been too complex for my first novel, so I dealt with one son at a time and built on the storyline as I went along. This allowed me to work with manageable subplots while building to the primary plot. It also let me explore the various locations, cultures, and characters involved. I am that writer who has taken ten years to complete a series. It is a very difficult undertaking when spread out over that amount of time. Not only is it easy to forget what threads are still dangling, but my writing style and ability changed significantly over those ten years. That makes it a challenge to maintain the series "voice."

Another reason for writing a series is "branding." Whether at the publisher's motivation or as a personal choice, writers develop series or universes to play in because they develop a following. The more opportunity you offer the reader to immerse themselves in a world they are familiar with, the more they seem to want of that world. The characters become cherished friends or mesmerizing foes. The setting becomes comfortable, and true fans thirst for a deeper understanding or greater detail. If the writer has done their job, the world becomes real, and people want more—readers because they have invested interest, the publishers because they want to capitalize on that interest.

The Difference between Series and Shared World

Both of these have existed for some time and have similar characteristics and methods of development. But let's look at some of the fundamental differences.

Series are often a natural development. A writer will either start out with a series in mind, or the story will grow beyond one book. (In some instances, the publisher decides one book should be broken into several, or that they want continuations of a solo book to create a series, but that is a marketing decision brought on by the bottom line.)

Shared Worlds are crafted specifically to establish a universe that an author or several authors can play in. It has many of the characteristics of a series except that the world's development generally comes from multiple sources. Again, this is for branding purposes. If multiple authors write in the same universe, it increases everyone's visibility, develops content quicker, and makes for a rich and varied backdrop for endless story possibilities. Novels and short stories often come out of such efforts, with everyone taking part in the profit based on their level of involvement or what content they developed that was utilized. This is a way to build a body of work and recognition without the level of effort a series by a solo author would take. If a shared world becomes popular, it can build an author's career.

The Dangers of Series Writing

Yeah, there is always a drawback, right? In this case, several…

Early Termination. If an author plans on a series, they invest time and effort in multiple volumes. Unfortunately, several things might happen to prevent all the books from being published, or even written.

- The publisher might elect not to publish subsequent books if those published did not do as well as they anticipated, but they still retain the rights, preventing the author from seeking publication for the full series elsewhere.

- The publisher might cease operation as a business.

- Due to some life event, the author does not complete all of the volumes in the series.

Creative Burnout. An author by choice or at the motivation of the publisher takes on a series project and, at some point, loses focus or inspiration, resulting in a rambling collection of stories that are linked but lose cohesion. Typically, this applies to the massive bodies of work that go beyond the number of volumes you can count on one hand. (An exception to this are those authors who break their series into groupings, smaller -logies set in the overall storyline and universe, but with their own personal story arcs.)

Boredom. An author finds themselves stuck when a series becomes popular enough that that is all anyone — publisher or reader — wants from them. They are so caught up in meeting the demand that they find it difficult to explore other, unrelated ideas they might have. At best, the author just doesn't want to do what they are doing anymore and stops. At worst, they keep going until it becomes obvious they don't want to do what they are doing anymore, reflecting in their writing.

The unfortunate result of all the above: the reader is left frustrated or disappointed. There is either a lack of closure when a series prematurely terminates, or a lack of love when one goes on too long.

Summing Up

Series can be fun, productive, and lucrative. They can also be a trap. Play, explore, milk it for all it's worth, but in doing so, don't sacrifice your creativity and the variety that makes what we do exciting. If you are going to do this, do it well, be organized and thorough, or stick with solo works where continuity is only relevant for the book's duration.

Above all, we do this to fulfill our passion. Nothing kills passion like an obligation. If you have a passion for a series or a shared world, by all means, pursue it, but be prepared to put in the effort it takes to do it justice. And therein lies the madness…

Laundry Lists and Info Dumps

(Originally published in The Writer's Toolbox, Allegory Magazine)

In gaming, there is a rule…

(Hey, pay attention. I am going somewhere here.)

There is a rule in gaming: If the GM didn't hear it, it didn't happen. This works pretty well in gaming. It keeps the players honest, makes them precise, and failing that, gives the GM something to work with to add a little excitement to a campaign as things tend to go not as expected when players are sloppy with their declarations.

Unfortunately, while applicable, the same rule doesn't work as well in writing all the time. Writers need to remember that when conveying information, it needs to be fluid, dynamic, and interesting enough to hold the reader's attention. Unlike in gaming, where it is necessary to give a concise list of steps involved in an action.

There are two ways that writers do their work a disservice when adding detail to their story. (Okay, there's probably way more than two, but these are the ones I'm concerned with today.)

Laundry Lists

Don't leave out steps. We've all been told that at one point or another, right? If you leave out steps, you end up with characters that put down a coffee cup they never picked up to begin with or some other confusing stumbling block to the logic and flow of your story. Of course, in their eagerness to not miss a step, some authors fall into the trap of the Laundry List. As far as I know, this is my term, so don't look at me cross-eyed if it's not familiar to you.

Now, let me explain. A Laundry List is when a writer gives a point-by-point account of the steps a character goes through in completing an action in a paragraph or even one sentence. Think of it as a bullet list. For example:

> Katy reached for the knob, turned it, and pulled the door open.

There is nothing wrong with this sentence, *per se*, but it is dry, slow reading, particularly if the author makes a habit of using this style throughout their work. Not only that, but it can create an uncomfortable pattern in the pacing. In this particular instance, it certainly makes more sense to say simply that Katy opened the door.

Now, this was just an example of a simple action. There are times when you want to expand on a series of related actions instead of contracting them. For example:

> Devin opened the car door, slipped inside, put his key in the ignition, and started the car.

In an instance like this, you could just contract:

> Devin got into the car and started the engine.

See, all the other steps are implied in the two actions you condensed to. Simple, not very interesting, but it gets the point across so you can move on to more important things. However, what if this *is* a pivotal point in the action. That is when you want to invoke an emotional response; you want to build the tension. In instances like that, you want to go for more, not less.

> Devin hurried toward the car. His gut clenched as he attempted to slide his key into the lock. It took three tries with the way his hand shook. He stopped and took a deep breath, then forced his hand to still. This time the key slid into the lock. As he got into the car and started the engine,

his mind already raced ahead to Cooper General, where they had taken Kara.

In this example, I have added more steps, but I also peppered it with physical and emotional responses and added details that made the excerpt a point of interest, which moves the plot forward.

Info-Dumps

Now I know everyone has heard of these. Heck, everyone is guilty of these! But do you know how to recognize one? For me, an info dump is when the author steps back from the story itself to provide a load of details or information. It can be about the setting or the society or pretty much anything, but it is provided in a solid block and generally in an omniscient perspective, rather than from your POV character's perspective. Usually, it is detail relevant to the story and that the reader needs to know, but it is presented in a way that interrupts the story instead of flowing with it. That means it's taking the reader out of the story as well. They lose the thread of the action to partake in a mini (or not so mini) lecture. You don't want that. When you break the pacing like that, you are increasing your chances of losing the reader. Info dumps are boring. They are like the commercial that interrupts the action scene in a television show.

> Simon galloped across the fields aiming for the secret pass leading through the hills. His gelding screamed defiantly at their pursuers. In response, the mounted archers loosed a volley of arrows.
>
> One creased Simon's shoulder, and he crouched lower, giving Duro the signal to run faster. The horse leveled out with a clatter of hooves until the distance between them and the king's men lengthened. They crested the hill well in advance of the enemy.
>
> On the far side of the crest spread the land of Trinnon. An independent state holding only uneasy neutrality toward King Grant's realm. Deceptively peaceful, the

land had all manner of protections woven into the very landscape. What appeared now as peaceful, windswept wheat fields could very well drain an intruder of every ounce of blood simply with the lashing of those stalks against unprotected skin. Even the ground itself, gently rolling as it seemed, was known to rise up and crush a man beneath its folds, were he not there with honest intent.

Okay... a pretty long example, but what can I say... hazard of being a writer.

The first two paragraphs are active and full of tension. Something is happening, and we really want to know if he gets safely away. Then BOOM! Info Dump. See, we need to know this information, but this really isn't the way to do it. The third paragraph just kills all the lovely tension we've built up, and it takes the reader out of the action. Not good.

There are two ways you can handle this. One, introduce this information sooner in the story, then just allude to what the reader already knows. As so:

> Simon had to reach Trinnon, where the enchanted land itself would rise against the intruders following him.

This assumes the reader already knows what the land is capable of. If that hasn't been set up yet in the story, you could handle it this way as well.

> They crested the hill well in advance of the enemy.
>
> On the far side of the mound spread the land of Trinnon. Simon did not relax as he entered the enchanted land from which his mother had come. He watched closely for the signs she had warned him of. Signs that the land prepared to attack. With care, he guided Duro around the fields of wheat, not out of care for the farmer's bounty, but knowing that should Trinnon decide he trespassed, those sheaves would slice his skin to the bone. Though their pace continued slow, Simon's gut clenched tighter as he watched the ground for signs it would rise up and swallow them whole, all the while wishing he could gallop clear

before the soldiers drew near enough to spy them. His shoulders tightened at the thought. His mother never said what Trinnon would do against an arrow.

He tightened his grip on Duro's sides and risked a bit more speed, praying to be out of bow range before the enemy caught up.

So... it took me more time and words to convey the same information, but I did it in such a way that the reader learned what I wanted them to know while still maintaining the tension of the scene and moving the plot forward. The best way to both spot and avoid an info dump is to stay in your character's head. Once you leave that place, it's like hitting the pause button on the story. Find a way to integrate the necessary information into the action. If a paragraph is nothing but information, you know you've lost the thread. Your POV character should be the filter through which all information is fed.

Summing Up

Fiction should be a tapestry of emotion, action, details, and dialogue... all woven together to create a whole (hopefully pleasing) picture. To accomplish that, you need to integrate things seamlessly and maintain the proper tension and flow for the type of scene you are writing. This is why you need to be aware of any Laundry Lists or Info Dumps and work toward transforming them, integrating the details they convey into the story instead of letting them act as interruptions. Now, there will be times when you just want to acknowledge an action that has taken place and move on, but always remember to keep it interesting for the reader, keep them immersed in the story, and keep the details integrated. Most importantly, everything that takes place or that the reader learns about should be filtered through a character's point of view. This immerses the reader in the story in a way random exposition cannot accomplish.

Our Tawdry Love Affair
with Language

Don't deny it. Don't pretend. We are all in love with words. Sometimes we are transported. Sometimes delighted, and yes, sometimes carried away.

It's easy to lose control when you are having such fun. The elegance of a phrase can easily blind us to what is and is not good prose. Unfortunately, at times, while we are having fun with language, the reader just wants to know what the heck is going on.

(Oh, stop pouting!)

There is a time for letting go and a time for reining yourself in. Your job: figure out when is when. Let me help you out. There are several questions you can ask yourself when you are reviewing what you have written:

- *Does it say what needs to be said?* Exercising your vocabulary is all well and good, but you have to keep in mind the objective of a scene and make sure you have chosen the right words for what you want to say and don't lose track of what you want to convey, to begin with. (In other words, make sure the words mean what you think they do, and don't forget to get to the point.)

- *Is it clear?* When we get grand with our words, there is a danger. We know what we had in mind, but if the flourishes are too grand, the reader might not be able to follow. When using words that are likely to be less familiar to the reader, make sure that you help define them through contextual references. If they missed the important point, all those pretty words were wasted, as was the scene. For instance, kine is a cool word for a cow, but if you don't make that clear, the reader is left wondering what that strange animal on the hill is rather than paying attention to the dragon swooping down to eat it.

- *Does it distract the reader from what is going on?* What is it you are trying to get across? Are you trying to immerse the reader in your world, or are you trying to give them the information they need to advance the story? When you are just setting a scene or building a character, your allotment of frivolous words increases; when a scene has a more specific purpose, you want to be a bit more stingy because the more emphasis you put on something, the more important the reader thinks it is so they might not pay attention where you want them to if there are too many things going on.

- *Does it slow down the pacing?* Fancy phrasing is not compact… you need time and space to be eloquent. The pace of a scene will slow down significantly the more intricate your prose becomes. Basically, you have two choices: relaxed or tense. The more words you use to say something, the less hurried the reader feels. So… describing a battlefield after the battle, explore every nuance you want; gearing up for the battle itself, keep the pacing — and the wordage — tighter than a miser's fist. The action has the wrong kind of impact if you don't build up to it, so pacing is an important part of literary tension. You want the reader to anticipate what is coming and feel the tension the characters do, so background details that are not relevant fade away, sentences get short and to the point so that while the reader is reading faster, they feel like they are rushing head-on into the action.

- *Is it appropriate?* What type of setting are you writing about? What are the characters like? If you get all fancy with the language when you are writing a story about street kids in East L.A., the poetry of your words is going to jar against what should be gritty images and settings. Let your vocabulary out to play, but make sure it gets along with your topic. Otherwise, the tone of your story is going to contradict the content.

Reality Check

After you are done evaluating your work against the above checklist, you have one more thing you can do to make sure your piece in harmony with itself and achieving its objective. Read it. Yes, read it… out loud!

(Okay, now you're just whining…)

The best way to catch conflicts in your own work is to read it out loud because you can hear the language and because it forces you to slow down and actually think about the words. Reading silently doesn't cut it because everything sounds perfect in your brain and your memory helpfully supplies any details you missed adding to the page. If you read aloud, it will emphasize those places where information is missing or where there is some disconnect between the language and the content, particularly in the dialogue. If a character is talking and you feel silly saying the words out loud, it is much worse than if the narrative sounds a little hokey.

Not comfortable reading yourself a story out loud? There are programs that can do it for you. Some of them might even already be on your computer, tablet, or smartphone.

Summing Up

Words can be wonderful, glorious, and a lot of fun to play with. They can evoke emotion, they can transport imaginations, they can create something out of nothing, but there has to be a synergy between tone, content, pace, and characterization. Play with the language all you want but don't lose sight of your purpose. For a writer, the language should never become more important than the story. When there is time, loosen your grip on those words and let them out, but be ready to knuckle down and get to the point so that the story flows to its conclusion naturally, rather than in meandering starts and stops.

Give Me A Break!
The Need for Literary Pauses

(Originally published in the Writer's Toolbox, Allegory Magazine.)

Have you ever listened to someone tell a story and you can't tell that they've taken a breath? They go on and on, and there is no break for you to interject a comment or to even digest what they've already told you. Besides making the teller seem like a bore, this also makes it difficult for the listener to appreciate the story being told.

Breaks take place for several reasons: To allow you to breathe, to allow someone else to speak, for effect, and to allow what has been said to be absorbed. The same goes for writing.

Taking A Breath

Have you ever found yourself writing, and things just seem to go on forever? What you are writing is relevant to the plot and needs to be there, but things just seem to drag. That's when you need to take a literary breath. Review your scene, looking for natural breaks in the actions or thoughts. It can really help your pacing if you feed the reader details in smaller bits.

Let me show you what I mean with the following literary tools:

Dialogue – depending on your usage, this allows you to break up long sections of exposition, show the interaction between characters, and share information from multiple sources. Dialogue takes you out of a single point of view and introduces the potential for conflict or cooperation. It is also a way to introduce an active component to an otherwise (potentially) static scene.

Example:

Kyle didn't know what he was going to do. Yesterday everything had been perfect: he was days away from graduation, his girlfriend Shelly had received her acceptance letter from the same college he was going to, and Dad had agreed to loan them his Mustang for the big graduation bash... Today? Armageddon.

Overnight the comfortable routine that was his reality disintegrated, casting him and everyone he knew adrift. No jobs, no school, no safe little communities. The cities were in ruin, and the countryside had dangers lurking everywhere: thieves, invaders, wild creatures no one could identify. Kyle had no idea where Shelly was or his mother. His dad was downstairs with Mr. Jenkins from next door, packing all the supplies they could readily carry.

Kyle's hands shook as he shoved climbing gear and his most rugged clothes into one backpack, and first aid supplies and other necessities from the upstairs bathroom into another. He tried not to think too hard about those who were missing, but he wasn't very successful. Where could they be? He wanted to get out there and look for them, but Dad said the first thing they needed to do was to get somewhere safe, where they could defend themselves before they tried to rescue anyone else.

"Son! Move, now!" his father called from the landing. "Mathson spotted shock troops heading this way!"

Shoving supplies in any which way, Kyle hurried to the stairs, taking them two at a time until he stood beside his father. Kyle swallowed hard and tried not to look as frightened as he felt. "Where will we go?"

"We're gathering everyone we can find out at the old mine," Dad answered. "With all those tunnels, they'll have a hard time finding us, and even if they do, there are more than enough ways out so we won't be trapped. Once we get everyone hidden away, we can concentrate on finding those who are missing."

Okay… so it's not a *great* example, but hey… I wrote it on the fly! In either case, basically, it serves its purpose. We have three paragraphs of just being in Kyle's head. Yes, he's doing stuff, and yes, he's thinking thoughts that give us important information, but it's all in isolation, and any threat is distant because he is, after all, just thinking about stuff. However, when his father interjects, all of a sudden, there is an active threat, character interaction, shared information, and a plan. Finally, something is *happening*. From a story mechanics standpoint, all of this serves to advance the plot, inform the reader, and increase the tension.

Underline for Emphasis – Okay… not literally, but let me explain what I mean. When you underline something, you set it off from the text around it. That tells the reader it is important. When you are writing fiction — or heck, even non-fiction — you can do the same thing with ideas. If there is a line or concept you want to impact the reader, you can give it a little punch by setting it off as its own paragraph.

Example:

Kyle didn't know what he was going to do. Yesterday everything had been perfect: he was days away from graduation, his girlfriend Shelly had received her acceptance letter from the same college he was going to, and Dad had agreed to loan them his Mustang for the big graduation bash…

Today? Armageddon.

Overnight the comfortable routine that was his reality disintegrated, casting him and everyone he knew adrift. No jobs, no school, no safe little communities. The cities were in ruins, and the countryside had dangers lurking everywhere: thieves, invaders, wild creatures no one could identify. Kyle had no idea where Shelly was or his mother. His dad was downstairs with Mr. Jenkins from next door, packing all the supplies they could readily carry into backpacks.

It is a small change but think of it as a dramatic pause. The way the original selection was written, all the same information was there, but it blended together, thought leading into thought. By setting off just those two words, they stand out and grip the reader. You don't want to do it too often, but there are definitely places where one-liners like this will have more impact when you let them stand on their own. It also helps to break up a pace that might be plodding along.

Scene (Section) Breaks

Sometimes, it is hard to know when to end a scene. After all, when you are writing in a linear fashion, things progress in a certain way, one idea leading to another. Life isn't a line, though. It's a tapestry. (I know, I know… I use that comparison an awful lot, but you know, if something applies…). With a tapestry, images are formed by bringing one thread to the forefront and then switching to another, repeating as needed until the picture is complete. As writers, it is our job to know when to cut away to present the reader with an intricately woven whole, rather than just a string of linked scenes.

There are several natural breaks writers can make use of:

Cliffhangers – something is about to happen, but the reader is left not knowing the ultimate outcome. This ramps up the tension and the interest, planting a need to know what happens next.

Bombshells – something unexpected happens, rattling the characters and changing the reader's expectations of where things are going. Again, this ramps up the tension and piques interest.

Slow fades – you can also think of this as a transition. Each scene should have one primary objective. Once that objective is achieved, it leaves a natural pause where another related scene can be interjected. In some instances, the next objective will be stated, in which case the scene break represents the passage of time as the characters position themselves for the next step. In other instances, the characters — and the reader — might be in the dark about what happens next, so the scene break represents the revealing of other factors that will impact their eventual actions.

Example:

"We're gathering everyone we can find out at the old mine," Dad answered. "With all those tunnels, they'll have a hard time finding us, and even if they do, there are more than enough ways out, so we won't be trapped. Once we get everyone hidden away, we can concentrate on finding those who are missing."

The room spun, and Kyle found himself breathing too fast. The mines. He'd always avoided the mines; they were dangerous. Dark and unstable, where an unseen gas could kill you in a few breaths, or rocks could fall from nowhere on the unsuspecting. Kyle's best friend had disappeared there long ago. What were the chances they would find what was left of him?

***

Beneath the school, there were catacombs, a massive version of the old bomb shelters from the fifties and sixties, where the threat of nuclear attack was the monster in everyone's closet. Most of the town actually had them, in their yards, beneath their businesses. Probably a lot of people had forgotten about them; heck, there were probably quite a few who didn't even know they were there.

Shelly wasn't one of those people.

See, for over twenty-four years, her father had been the custodian of the high school. Her mother had died giving birth to her, and Papa couldn't afford a sitter, so Shelly had grown up with the school as her playground. When the invasion happened, she had been in the choir room practicing a song she was to sing during the graduation ceremony. There had been explosions and screams, and every light in the building went out. In the chaos that ensued, Shelly had gathered everyone she could find and led them into the catacombs.

This is more of an example of the first two types of breaks, but you get the idea (don't you?). This scene break accomplishes several things: it builds the tension by ending the first scene on a traumatic memory, it allows the reader to take a "breath," and the new scene both introduces a primary character mentioned previously and gives the reader information Kyle didn't have about what happened to her. That helps to progress the plot as different variables are brought into play and, hopefully, draws the reader into the story as they come to know the characters and become interested in what happens to them.

Chapter Breaks

These are pretty much like mega scene breaks, which means all of the above applies. The real difference is in the transition. Mostly, there are two primary types of chapter breaks:

Perspective - This is where the same scene continues in the next chapter, but generally with a different focus character. The switch in point of view allows you to have a different slant on what is happening and lets you explore events from inside a different character's head. Sometimes this is just to have a fresh perspective… a change of mental scenery, as it were. Other times, there is information the reader needs to know that can only be gained by switching focus. Example:

> The room spun, and Kyle found himself breathing too fast. The mines. He'd always avoided the mines; they were dangerous. Dark and unstable, where an unseen gas could kill you in a breath, or rocks could fall from nowhere on the unsuspecting. Kyle's best friend had disappeared there long ago. What were the chances they would find what was left of him?
>
> ***
>
> Chapter 2
> Not bothering to hide his concern, James watched his son closely. He knew what he was asking would be difficult for the boy, but what other option did they have?

There was nowhere safe for them, nowhere else to hide, that he could think of. Reaching out, he clasped Kyle's shoulder, trying to reassure him. He was a good kid, but could he handle what they were about to face? When his son took a deep breath and nodded in silent acceptance, James let his pride in the boy seep into his gaze a moment, then he grabbed three of the five packs on the table and led the way to the back door.

The power was out, and the sky was overcast, so there was no light to betray them, but as he scanned the darkness for any sign of movement, he had to wonder if that mattered. After all, what did they know of these shock troops and what they were capable of?

The action continues in a mostly continuous line, but the change in perspective gives the reader a different insight into the situation and the characters involved.

Break-Away – This is when the writer breaks away to a completely unrelated scene. It is a way to further weave together the plots and subplots of longer fiction by alternating scenes only loosely related in the overall plot, touching on characters or events that will eventually converge, but not yet.Example:

The room spun, and Kyle found himself breathing too fast. The mines. He'd always avoided the mines; they were dangerous. Dark and unstable, where an unseen gas could kill you in a breath, or rocks could fall from nowhere on the unsuspecting. Kyle's best friend had disappeared there long ago. What were the chances they would find what was left of him?

***

Chapter 2

The air was thin and harsh, the colors of the landscape soothing one instant, brash and jarring the next. General Aoki curled back his jowls in distaste as he glowered at his surroundings, looking for a hint of movement that would betray the pathetic vermin infesting this place. They were proving surprisingly difficult to suppress, despite their inferior physical capabilities. One had to search vigilantly to find them.

There. There was a flicker at the extreme corner of his vision. Without turning, Aoki motioned his subaltern forward.

"Sir?" the soldier responded, his eyes lowered in deference.

"The structure behind us at your shield side," the general answered, "have a squad clear the vermin from the upper level."

The subaltern dropped to one knee, his head bowed, before straightening and moving off to carry out his orders.

The action following the chapter break is only in the broad sense related to the characters in the previous scene, so it calls for more of a hard division between the two. This type of break fills in details needed later to weave the story more tightly together.

Summing Up

So as you can see, there are nearly as many ways to pause a storyline as there are reasons to do so. The examples and instances I have shared with you here are by no means complete, but I hope they are sufficient to illustrate my point and get you thinking about natural breaks, both how to recognize them and when to implement them. Life is full of them... commercials, halftime shows, choruses. No matter the venue or the form of entertainment, our appreciation is often amplified by a pause of some sort. Learn to use those pauses to your advantage; after all... no one likes a bore, so give the reader a break and take a breath once in a while ;)

Don't Forget the Rule Book:
Authors

You can fool yourself all you want, but if there is one thing in life that never changes, it's that there is *always* a rulebook, both for you and your characters. Now, I'm not saying all of you will follow it—you should, but I'm not that naïve.

Let me explain to you why fiction requires rules both in the writing and in the story. I'm not talking grammar and stuff like that. (If you haven't learned why we need that in storytelling, I doubt I am the one to drive the lesson home.) No, this article is about the necessary boundaries in your literary universe. Because let's face it, that is all that rules are. They tell us how far we can go before there are—or should be—consequences.

(Believe me... I know consequences.)

Rules for the Author

Identify Your Characters. If the reader is to care about the characters in your story, they have to know them. Their name, their history, what they look like. How much detail you go into will depend on how important the character is. You don't have to reveal everything at once, but don't delay too long, either. There will be times when you have a legitimate reason for withholding detail, but if it is a primary character and you aren't writing a mystery or suspense, the only good reason for not giving at least the name of your character right off the bat is because your character doesn't *know* who they are—or doesn't want anyone *else* to know who they are. You should make some effort to establish the basics early on because if you don't, the reader will form their own impression, and it might not synch up with what you reveal later on. Basics: Name, gender, age, hair, eyes, and skin tone.

Maintain a Timeline. The more complex your storyline, the more important this rule is. You have to keep track of the details so that things happen in the proper order. If a character needs a particular item to achieve the story's main objective, make sure you provide a scene of them finding or claiming that item, or establish that is something they already have. It is not unheard of to stagger threads in a story so that you are taking two steps forward in one scene and one step back to an earlier time with a different character for the next scene, but if you do this, you have to make it clear or else you jog the reader out of the story as they try and follow the progression.

Pre-Establish Resources. Again, to recycle an example, if certain things will be needed to ensure your character's success — even if they aren't aware of it yet — you need to make the reader aware of the item or ability or whatever it is in some manner. That the character has it in their possession, knows its existence, or learns about it in advance of actually needing it. Unless, of course, part of the goal is to find that item, then you could build suspense by having them attempt their goal, not succeed, and then learn why, thus sending them off on another adventure before the tale is done. Whatever you do, you do not want to arrive at the challenge, reveal that something is needed, and have the character either conveniently have it or suddenly find it right there…

Keep Things Straight. You have to keep the details you've already written consistent throughout the story. Don't contradict yourself, don't make your character's eyes brown, then ten pages later tell us they are as blue as the noonday sun. If you confuse the details, you confuse your readers, and then they won't enjoy the story, and maybe not even finish it if you are sloppy too often. The same goes for the order of events, emotional reactions, etc. Remember what you wrote, or you could contradict yourself later, and your story will no longer make sense, to one degree or another. Even small details can throw things off, and believe me, the readers will notice. Can't tell you the number of times I've flipped back to the beginning of the book to make sure I wasn't reading wrong... and oops, there goes the story; I'm not in it anymore, I'm hunting down particulars.

Don't Push Plausibility. Yes, it is fiction, yes something particular has to happen, but it is your job as the author to make things make sense. That means building in the steps that lead to your ultimate end so that the reader can follow where you were going with things and say "yes, that could happen," even if the story is fantastical, because you have done the footwork. Some things to avoid: Making things too easy for your characters, leading them through the story in a straight line, disregarding time and space in relation to what is happening, etc.

Establish Your Own Rules. Unless you are writing in a universe you've played in many times before, you are likely to figure out your current world as you go along, which means you have to figure out the rules. What social, environmental, or other obstacles does your character have to face? Maybe you have a world where women are forbidden to touch the ground in public, so rich women are carried everywhere on litters, and poor women have to ride on their husband's backs, or maybe gravity works in reverse, or all blue-eyed beings are insane... except for the alien who just arrived from Earth... only no one knows. Give structure to your world that will both define it and challenge your characters because all stories need conflict... something to overcome.

Summing Up

Have you read something and thought, 'Oh! Come on! Like that would happen,' or 'Please, the character is being so stupid! Give them a backbone!'? Or have you found yourself confused about who is doing what, when, in a story? Authors have a lot more to keep in mind than personality and plot points. Logic and physics and temporal continuity are not just the things of science fiction movies. When you are writing fiction, you are building worlds. Even if it looks unsurprisingly similar to the one we walk around in every day, you still have to do a good job putting that world together so that the reader can get lost in it for a while. The more effort you put into your world's foundation, the more the reader will enjoy themselves because there will be a complex backdrop complementing the story you are telling. Don't get sloppy because you think the background details aren't as important as the primary action. Think about it... it's the difference between a multi-million dollar Hollywood set and the painted backdrop from your fifth-grade play. Which would you prefer to have your characters parade in front of?

Don't Forget the Rule Book: Characters

For good or ill, everyone needs rules… if nothing else, so they have something to break.

But seriously now, we really do need them. That goes for your characters just as much as it goes for you and I. (I can hear the whine right now: but *Whhhyyy*?)

Good fiction is propelled by two things: Goals and Conflict. Both basically boil down to "something the main character needs to achieve or overcome." For your character's journey to be interesting, they need barriers to pit themselves against, proving their skill and worth, as it were.

Let's face it, if it's too easy, it's almost always dissatisfying.

Now, since this article is all about the rules, let's take a look at the various kinds you can throw at your hero to plop him in the middle of interesting times.

The Rules of Nature

In many instances, most of us choose to fall back on what we know: birds fly, things fall down, etc. Nice, simple, familiar to both the author and the reader. No one has to think much about it. But if you are writing genre fiction, you get to change those rules by putting your characters in settings that would never occur on our quaint little mudball. When that happens, you have to consider what makes *there* different from *here* and what impact that will have on your characters.

Predators. Let's face it, if you have invented a predator, it is for two reasons: 1) your character is going to encounter it, or 2) your character has to avoid it. Predators can take the form of animals or sentient beings—I know... state the obvious, why don't I—as well as mundane or supernatural.

Things to consider when creating predators:

- What threat do they pose?
- What are their habits?
- What is their territory/natural environment?
- How do they attack?
- What is their weakness?
- What is their goal?
- What defenses are there against them?

Environment. You might be asking, how is environment a rule?

(Oh, don't pretend... I know that's what you're thinking. Don't worry, I have an answer to that.)

In more complex stories, particularly genre fiction, the setting is a character in and of itself. It is the writer's job to figure out how the environment will interact with the hero to either help or hinder the journey. Where a character may go and how difficult the journey is dictated by the environment. For example:

- There may be dangerous storms in one area, treacherous terrain in another.
- The air near the mountains might be unbreathable due to gases escaping from deep within the planet (just saying...).
- The path to the ultimate goal of the story might run right across an enemy border.
- Quests might require a difficult, dangerous, or arduous journey that must be followed religiously to achieve success.

There are many written and unwritten rules related to geography that influence a character's path, each with its own level of risk. The writer must determine the risks and provide viable reasons why the characters avoid or confront those risks.

Now, I'm not saying to create pitfalls just to have pitfalls. Any obstacle the characters encounter should serve more of a purpose than just getting in their way. Generally, this takes the shape of some geological feature or location that is dangerous for various reasons and just happens to be smack dab in the middle of where the main character and their friends need to go. Your task as the writer is to make these features challenging and threatening without making them seem hopeless. There must be some potential for escape, no matter how slim.

Personality. Each person has internal rules of behavior, their own gauge for determining what is and is not acceptable. One of the greatest methods of creating conflict in a story is to force a character to act outside those rules. The lesser of two evils, as it were. Crisis of conscience is a common method of building tension into a story; work it with a gentle hand and balance it carefully with the impression you want to give the reader of the character. Let's face it… if you want the reader to be sympathetic to the character, it is harder to fudge these types of rules. Once you establish what a character does or does not consider acceptable behavior, you have to maintain that personality if you want to hold the reader.

The Rules of Society

So, above, we dealt with rules that just are; now we move on to imposed or implied rules. Any group where individuals live in close proximity — either animal or sentient — has its idea of what is and is not acceptable. Some are guided by instinct, others by experience, yet others by a desire for power and control. No matter how dumb a rule might seem, it originated from some specific situation that someone determined was unacceptable, thus leading to the regulation and enforcement of the desired behaviors. Here… let me break it down further:

Social. You've heard the phrase, "It's just not done," yes? Well, these are the unofficial rules. That means they are not legally binding but carry consequences determined by the community or social grouping a person belongs to or interacts with. There is generally — but not always — a logical reason for the development of these rules. For example, a century or two ago, it was expected a man would always walk on the outside when walking with a lady down the street, a social convention that developed from the fact that people used to dump their chamber pots out the window into the gutter. With the man on the outside (street side), he protects the woman from being doused with waste. Other conventions develop more out of social class than an actual desire to protect individuals (such as one man slapping another man in the face with a glove over some slight (perceived or actual) requiring both men to duel). And finally, a need for self-defense accounts for other unspoken rules, such as the reason we drive on the right side of the road... originally, it was horse-drawn wagons in the Old West, and the pioneers kept to the right when passing opposing traffic so they could have a clear shot with their guns to defend themselves if needed.

   Some things to consider when devising social rules for your world or culture:

- Are there classes or castes?

- Are there distinctions between what is acceptable determined by gender, class, or some other defining factor?

- What are the living conditions that would lead to the rule in question?

- What are the consequences of violating these social mores?

   Generally, these are rules with less serious repercussions in the bigger scope of things. Perhaps they result in a bad reputation, social shunning, a fight with the offended party, or even exclusion from the community in some manner or degree. They might make life uncomfortable, but not usually very harsh and not anything extreme. Offenses that carry a higher consequence generally transition into law, which leads us, naturally, to legal rules...

Legal. Legal rules can have two objectives: Protect or Control. In theory, and in an ideal society, most laws are instituted to protect people and property from others' inappropriate acts. Examples would be:

- Livestock must be penned to prevent them from trampling people or damaging property.

- People must have insurance when they drive to ensure they can pay for damages or injury should they cause an accident.

- Sidewalks must be kept in good repair to prevent pedestrians from tripping and hurting themselves.

Of course, who lives in an ideal society? There are plenty of rules that come out of a desire to control. Mostly these are zoning laws, at least in the modern-day, but they give you the idea:

- Cars may not be parked on the grass.

- Two-hour parking limit only.

- No liquor to be sold on Sundays (or before noon, or whatever variants there are.)

Religious. Faith-based rules may or may not overlap with Legal or Social, depending on the society you are developing or using as a foundation for your made-up world. In theory, these rules develop out of religious texts passed down by clergy communing with the worshiped deity. In reality, human drives often influence the dictates of religion as much as theology does. (There is a — *ahem* — fine tradition of religion being used as a power base rather than a true calling.) Examples of religious rules:

- Don't eat meat on Fridays.

- Don't drink of the fruit or the grain (alcohol).

- A woman does not show her hair/face/etc. in public.

The level of consequence for violating such religious rules is determined by the amount of power held by the given religious institution and what role they play in the government.

Historically, punishments ranged from being denied food, briefly incarcerated, or even put to death.

Overcoming the Rules

Since it is bad form to have a conflict that your characters have no hope of overcoming, you have to consider how that can plausibly be achieved. Simple enough to do. Here are a few examples:

- Give your character a super-skill, some ability that makes them particularly suited to circumvent the rule in question or that makes it not apply.

- Have an object or talisman that can be obtained that will help the hero achieve what needs to be done.

- Give the character a hand… or several, by writing in support characters that have a skill that will help overcome the conflict(s) faced through combined effort and cooperation.

- Develop a benefactor who can smooth the way if the infraction is discovered.

- If the obstacle (rule) is environmental in nature, write in some other natural feature that would allow the character to overcome the obstacle if they are ingenious enough to recognize its usefulness.

Living with the Consequences

Sometimes there will be no way to circumvent the rules. Hey… it happens, in both real life and in fiction. And each time it does, everyone has a choice whether to respect the rules or break them. That means there are going to be times your characters chose wrong. Maybe it is because of a moment of weakness or ignorance, or maybe it is because the consequences of *not* breaking the rule are worse. Don't be afraid for your characters to take a fall now and then… temporary or otherwise.

Summing Up

I'm sure I haven't covered everything here, but you get the idea. Basically, when it comes down to it, rules in fiction exist so the author can find a way around them, adding tension, excitement, and action to a tale to propel the plot forward (and entertain the reader). In other words... as writers, we need to make our characters work for it, whatever "it" is. After all, readers don't want a walk through the park... they want a Navy SEALs obstacle course, something tough enough that it seems it might almost be too much for the hero. Almost. Very important to remember the "almost."

Cut the Bull – Energy Boosters for Writing

You know, sometimes we just don't know when to stop. No. It's true, even I'm guilty (I know. *Shocker*.) We get so caught up in the language and discovery of these worlds in our heads that we just pile on the detail. We get so caught up in the creativity that we have to build the universe right down to the thumbtacks on the wall, or we're worried about not being clear or missing something important until we end up with a literal checklist of all the steps that took our characters from A to B… for each scene.

Okay, so perhaps I exaggerate, but not completely. There are times in fiction that call for expansive detail, and others where too much clutter kills the action. It is important to know how and when to hold back. Ask yourself a few questions while you're writing:

Have we been here before? If this is the first time your character is in this setting, the reader needs to know something about the surroundings. It helps shape their mental image of where they are. If you don't give them detail, they start to imagine things on their own, and that can screw you up later when you *are* specific about a character or setting.

Now it is tempting to just give a paragraph with all the details and then go on to the character, but in most instances, that gives a choppy, disjointed feel to a scene, kind of like the difference between beads on a string as opposed to a smooth braid where things are neatly woven together. I like braids. It is better to feed the reader details in relation to the character and their actions. As the character notices or experiences aspects of the space, that is when you introduce them. It keeps things fluid, connected, and gives a sense of discovery, rather than of being told something.

If the character has been in a particular setting before, you want to focus on what is relevant to the character, the action, or a future point in the plot at that very moment, and not a lot of extraneous detail that will distract the reader from what is important in the scene.

What is the point of the scene? The answer to that determines how much detail is appropriate. Sometimes you want to feed things in piecemeal. Other times you HAVE to go in-depth.

- *Is this a destination or a transition?* If the answer is a destination, we need to know stuff. What does the place look like, who and what are where? If this is just a transition to someplace more important, any details you give should be important.

- *Is it taking too long to get where you're going?* Are you trying to build tension or move from one part of the plot to another? If so, and you, as the writer, start to feel it is taking forever, take a look at the details you have included. Some things are important for plot or character, but extraneous stuff should be kept to a minimum until you hit a more relaxed portion of the story or book.

- *Is this relevant later?* Sometimes you have to include detail, no matter what the scene. There are always points that you have to reveal the bits and pieces that come together later so that everything makes sense, like mentioning a belt dagger if the character uses it three chapters later to save himself, or noticing a peculiar tattoo on a passerby that seems irrelevant but in the end betrays the villain.

- *What actions propel the plot?* When it comes to the things the characters do, some steps are unavoidable, but others you can skip over. We don't need to know that Jim opened the drawer, took out a pair of socks, closed the drawer, sat on the bed, and then put on the socks. Suffice it to say, Jim took socks from his dresser and put them on. On the other hand, if Jim is fighting an olfactory-sensitive monster and the only thing that can save him is the month-old dirty socks under his bed, making him work to retrieve them in excruciating detail serves a purpose.

When it comes down to it, we must all judge each piece we write by how much the detail adds to the story or how much the detail sucks the life out of it. If you aren't sure, read the work aloud, feel the pacing of it. If a snail could move faster, trim things down. If you reach the end and you have no clear picture of where you are or how you got there, slow down a bit and explore the world you're creating because that is how the reader comes to care, when you make the world and those that populate it real for them.

Structural Assists to Pacing

I know most of this article has had to do with content, but I wanted to mention several ways to use your writing structure to impact the scene's pace. These are the conscious choices you can make to inspire subconscious responses in your readers. Wonderful tools when used properly.

Chop it Up. A great way to increase the tension and pacing of a scene is to use short sentences or even sentence fragments (sparingly, please.) to give a sense of urgency and action. A key place to use this is a fight scene where what is happening is most important. Such as:

Jim dove left. Claws raked his feet but didn't take hold. Thud. His body hit the floor. Air left his lungs. Spots formed before his eyes. Yet instinct sent him rolling out of the way. A massive paw slammed down where he'd been. He rolled again. Scrambled for the safety of beneath the bed. The creature snarled. Its nose wrinkled and twitched.

Violently. Jim spied last month's socks just out of reach and knew what to do.

You get the idea…

Punch the Line. No… don't pick a fight with it. The words would win. Okay, let me explain. Sometimes a point you make in a story is like a sucker punch. Unexpected or profound enough to really grab the reader, but somewhat lost among the other copy. Now, this is another thing you don't want to overuse, but you can get a lot of mileage out of taking that perfect line and letting it stand on its own. Here's an example from my novel, *Today's Promise* (eSpec Books, 2020):

> Looking around the room, she noticed another bed, that one holding a young woman deathly pale and covered in dust. Another woman Agnieszka didn't recognize was tenderly cleaning her up.
>
> The sight left Agnieszka feeling empty and alone. She had had enough. Confirming her own person was free of dust and rebraiding her hair, she felt marginally closer to civilized.
>
> TIME TO REJOIN THE HUMAN RACE.
>
> And she stepped out of the room. There were a number of people waiting there, half of them looking like they'd just come from battle. Again with the dust, and a bit more blood. She swept the group with her gaze. She knew two of them. Agnieszka turned to the young man who she'd first encountered at her own cottage. Back before her life went catawampus. She didn't even know his name, but of the two faces she recognized, he was the one she mistrusted the least.
>
> "Take me home, now."

No, the line isn't printed all in caps in the book. Just highlighting my example. That line could have easily been run into the paragraph preceding it, but popping it out has much more impact.

Summing Up

Writing is one choice after another. What to say and how to say it, heck, even when. Consider your options to achieve the best effect, keeping the reader interested and moving forward to the next page at the proper pace for what's going on. Use every trick you have to increase your work's (positive) impact, but always remember to include the lulls, the relaxed moments, the times when it is natural to stop and smell… anything. And when it's time to get tense… let the world fade into the background, so all the reader's attention is riveted where it belongs.

Getting to the Root of the Matter

You know, history is important. History is a connection, a foundation, roots. Yeah, cliché, but true.

I've had my own personal encounter with history recently. I can't tell you how exciting it was to discover another branch of my family, to know there was more there than I knew. I'd always been curious but in an incidental, back-of-the-mind kind of way. The more and more I learn, the more I realize how important it is to know where I come from. This is why I feel moved to write on this topic right now because I have had a quite real experience with the importance of knowing where people — yourself in particular — come from. See, growing up, I didn't know much family history. We weren't close geographically, much of the family documentation was lost through several rounds of fires, and many of my family's elders had passed well before I understood the concept of family history. I think I am not alone in this.

Maybe that is the cause of the social disconnect many of us experience today. Family just doesn't seem to mean as much as it used to. We are unrooted, and so we drift and wander and lose our place in the structure.

Now you might be wondering what that has to do with writing, am I correct? Let me tell you.

We might be a society with loose roots, but that doesn't mean that we don't want them! We want to feel connected, anchored, as if we have a place. Consequently, that means we want the same for those we care about, and if you've done your job as a writer, you and your readers care about your characters.

There is satisfaction in knowing the history exists, even if you don't know all the details. Characters with a history are rooted in their world, an integral part of it. To put it simply, they matter. We want the characters to matter. When you have a character that just sort of drifts through their reality without impact beyond the immediate events, in the back of your mind, you wonder what was the point? (Oh! Come on... yes, you do! We all do.)

The Social Footprint

Have you ever pulled up a plant? Not talking a weed or a blade of grass, or the mums once they've died and turned into a hollow, papery brown stalk. Pull up an iris or a lily, or any number of perennial plants, and you'll notice that what appears to be a completely separate plant shares roots with those next to it, or even feet away! People are like that, which means your characters should be like that too.

There has been a lot of talk in recent years about carbon footprints, humanity's impact on the ecological world. I've come to realize that people also have a social footprint. It's measured in memories and documents and other assorted data. Videotapes and audio recordings. All of the little captured details of our lives are our roots because each one is a lasting documentation of our impact on the world in whatever degree... large, small, personal, sensational. It's how those that follow know we've been here, who we're connected with, and what we've done.

(Yeah, yeah... I know, not always a good thing!)

Now I'm not saying to put the informational equivalent of cement shoes on your characters, forcing them to drag their way through the story you are trying to tell. Some background detail is good, but too much kills a story. The reader doesn't have to know *everything* about *every* character, only what pertains to the story, except for maybe a little extra on your primary characters to flesh them out and make them real. After all, you are building a world, and worlds are cluttered.

You, however, are not the reader. You need a better understanding of those whose story you are telling.

Think about your characters, what has made them the way they are. Here are some questions you can kick around:

Who is my character related to? Maybe relevant, maybe not for your particular story, but the presence of parents and siblings and extended family impacts the way we develop. How we get along with those people has even more of an impact.

Where does my character come from? Family history and status is one of the biggest influences on our lives. It can determine how we perceive ourselves and how society perceives us (or how we think society perceives us, which can be even more relevant), what resources we have to draw upon and what skills we are likely to know just as a result of growing up, rather than specialized training.

What has happened to my character in the past? We learn from experience. (I know... I know... state the obvious, why don't I?) There is no way we are not impacted in some way by the events of our past. It colors how we respond and react to everything that comes after in some way. We are the sum of our experiences, and so should our characters be.

What does my character want to achieve? Our goals are very important in defining who we are and what we do. Whether it is directly related to the story's plot or not, the same goes for our characters.

It is up to you how much effort and time you put into figuring out a history for your characters, but there are several ways this helps you:

Continuity – By figuring out as many details as you can in advance and updating them as you go along, it gives you a reference you can check as you are writing to keep things straight and avoid conflicting information as you go. This is helpful for single book projects, but vital – in my opinion – for multi-book projects, take it from me. By book three, you're pulling your hair out trying to remember things.

Connectivity – No... we're not talking electricity or internet access. We're talking about those roots I mentioned earlier... the ones on the lilies and irises that connect plant to plant. Well, the more you know about your characters and the ways they are connected to each other, the more you can make use of that as you are writing to both tighten the story and employ your characters and their interactions with one another to reveal important details in a manner that feels natural.

Familiarity – The more you know about your characters, the better you understand their place in the reality you are building. The more you understand from the start, the less you have to puzzle out as you go along. I'm not saying things won't change, but it gives you a place to start from.

Depth – Whether you put the character details you figure out in the story or not, they help flesh out the character in your mind. If you know why they are doing things and how they are likely to respond for various reasons, it solidifies their personality. Eventually, you might use that background, and maybe you won't, but that doesn't mean it doesn't influence the story by giving you a greater understanding of the characters you are dealing with.

Summing Up

Don't take me wrong here; I'm not saying this is the way you must do things. I know better than that. Everyone's process is different, and what works for one person can completely bollox up the next. What I am saying, though, is whatever manner you choose, it is important to give some thought to your characters and how they relate to their surroundings. Understanding them gives you a clearer sense of where your story is going.

Profiling for Writers

(Originally published in the Writer's Toolbox column, Allegory Magazine.)

No! Not that kind of profiling! Character profiling. After all, when you write fiction, you aren't just conveying the details of a series of events. No. You are introducing the reader to your characters… your babies. Don't you think you should know who they are first?

When I give a workshop, I recommend writers create character sheets when they get started, mostly — but not exclusively — for their primary characters. Gamers do this all the time; it is how they keep track of what their characters look like, some history, and what they can do. It allows them to follow the game (story) the game master is running without being bogged down with trying to remember everything about their character. It also allows them to modify the details as the character grows and learns, acquires possessions, or gets injured. It also makes it easier for them to maintain continuity from game campaign to game campaign, no matter how much time has passed in between. Face it, a character sheet is a condensed version of a life.

As writers, we can adapt that process. Heck, I actually have friends that literally roll up their characters using gaming manuals as guides. The basic details, anyway, particularly for secondary characters. Not saying you have to go that far, but the tracking aspect of the process is something we could all benefit from. Things you might want to consider in advance:

Name – give your characters a full name, first, middle, last, and nickname. You might not use all of them throughout the story, but it gives the character shape and personality. And it starts those threads of connection. Besides, who knows when the information might be useful!

Physical Description – readers like characters they can picture in their minds. To do that, they need things like hair and eye color, flesh tone, height, and weight. The more attention you pay to details, the more real that image is going to be. It also fixes the character in your own mind, so you understand what the character is capable of physically or what type of self-image they might have. Don't get me wrong, though. I'm not saying to lay several paragraphs on the reader at once going into excruciating detail about what each character looks like, but you can weave in threads of description as things are happening without slowing down the pace too much.

Intangibles – If you are familiar with role-playing games—of the D&D variety! Come on, keep it clean… well, unless you're writing erotica, then I guess you kind of can't—anyway, as I was saying, in RPGs, some characteristics are not visible, though the effects are. Things like dexterity, charisma, luck… establishing such details, even if it is only for your own clarification, will help enliven your character as you find places to bring these characteristics into evidence. A stumble here, a giggling starry-eyed girl there, happening upon just the thing needed to propel the story forward (without it seeming as if it happened by the Hand of Author) that will develop more fluidly as you write if you have an understanding of your character, to begin with.

Relationships – Unless you are writing a sequel or in an established universe with existing characters, you might not know in advance all the particulars of each character, or even your main characters, particularly if you are, like me, a pantser, but the nice thing about creating a character sheet is that you can go back later and fill in the gaps. If you know family details or the history between individual characters, make a brief note about the particulars on the relevant character sheets. It helps you keep things straight and also is a resource for figuring out who you can recruit for various tasks later on as the story develops.

Skills – It isn't enough to know what someone looks like. You need to know what abilities they have. Can they ride a bike? Do they know how to use a gun? Did their mother make them take ballroom dancing classes for ten years? You never know what will develop in a story; if your character starts out with certain skills, write them down; if skills surface while you are writing or the character learns something on the fly, write it down. And just as important, note if there are skills they are particularly bad at as well. These come in handy for two things... comic relief and building tension.

The How-To's

There are many methods for tracking characters, from paper to Microsoft Word files to computer programs such as Scriveners (http://www.literatureandlatte.com/scrivener.php) that allow a writer to organize every aspect of a writing project.

In the beginning, I mentioned character sheets, like you would use for a role-playing game. If you want to adapt a gaming character sheet for your purposes, you can likely find examples online, or there are usually blank sheets in the back of gaming manuals. If you don't want to go through the bother of hunting one down, you can just use sheets of paper, index cards, or an electronic file on your computer.

Layout - Think of the information sheet you fill out when you go to the doctor or apply for a job. Name and vital statistics are at the top, followed by more explicit details and history below. For story-specific events (those that develop as you write), start a timeline or a bullet list on the back.

Detail – you can go into as little or as much detail as you like, but keep in mind that you already wrote down what happened as the story developed. What you want here are the cliff notes on the key events and characteristics. For example, if they met someone on the train once, you probably don't have to record that, but if the person they met on the train was the villain that killed their father, then yeah, good idea to make a note of when they first met.

Photographs/Drawings – Not saying you have to do this, but I've known both gamers and writers alike who either draw a representation of their character or find an image online or in a magazine that is a rough approximation of how they envision the character to look. For them, it makes the character more "real," and they are better able to describe physical attributes as they are writing with that example before them.

Summing Up

I've said it before, and I'll no doubt will say it again; I'm not writing this to say that this is the way you should go about creating and tracking your characters, merely presenting a possible method, explaining the reasoning, and giving you some idea of how to go about it. The important thing here is not how you establish the particulars about your characters but the fact that you should.

Think about it, if someone tells you a story about someone one you know, it's both easier for you to follow and more likely you will be interested; if they tell you a story about a stranger, the less you can identify with the subject of the story the less you care.

Writers need the reader to care about their characters. However you do it, it's your job to make sure they do.

Jerking Tears and Tugging Heartstrings – Baiting the Emotional Hook

(Originally printed in The Writer's Toolbox: Allegory Magazine)

So what?
What's the big deal?
Why should I care?

You think you're the only one asking those questions? Think again. Every time a reader picks up a book, that's what's in the back of their minds. As the writer, it is your job to make sure the answers are on the page because that keeps them turning.

Think of it like this: if you're at a party and someone starts to tell you a story you don't care anything about, what do you do? Yeah... you either make an excuse to walk away, or you tune them out, making meaningless sounds of acknowledgment from time to time to make it seem like you're actually listening. Readers are the same way. If they don't care, they don't keep reading (unless it is schoolwork... then they get the *Cliff Notes* and read those).

Face it, you need the reader to *care,* and since we relate to the world through our emotions, that means there needs to be some emotional connection made between the reader and what is happening on the page.

Sometimes excitement will do that on its own, but not for long. You can't really maintain constant action in a story without losing... well... the story, and the reader for that point.

So, how do you inspire an emotional connection without giving a running commentary on how each character feels? Glad you asked...

Visible Physical Cues

Yeah... you've heard it before: "Show, don't tell." It is the easiest, least obtrusive way to inspire a response in your reader because it draws on their own experiences to provide the content that connects with the physical effects of emotion... the shudder, the clench, the frown, etc. For example:

> Tammy was angry.

Simple enough. Definitely clear. But lacking something. To what degree was she angry? How did she respond to the feeling? How did she express it?

> Tammy's lips pursed, and her forehead tightened in a scowl. She glanced away, not meeting his eye as a muscle in her cheek twitched.

See, the first example gives us information, but it's flat. There is no dimension to it. Whereas the second example resonates; it calls up memories of how the reader might have felt faced with a like situation, when they may have reacted in ways similar to the character. There is an intensity to such memories that transcends a mere statement of fact.

Most people reveal emotions by what they do before they even say a word. In fact, often, the physical cues are more honest and informative than anything they tell you. Not because everyone is dishonest, but because we typically grow up with two under-standings: emotions are vulnerability, and emotional displays are impolite. Because of this, we don't always let our emotions loose. (Yes, I know, this doesn't go for everybody. Some people thrive on emotional displays. But it's true enough.) Because of this, we have learned to put more faith in the physical signs of feeling, those unconscious, sometimes uncontrollable indicators. In gambling, they call it a "tell." Sometimes they are obvious, sometimes subtle.

Because this is how we interact with our world and gauge our encounters with others, employing that in our writing establishes a connection between the reader and the characters.

Internal Reactions

Emotions are messy.

(Yeah… tell you something you didn't know, right?)

Because of that, for various reasons, we internalize a lot of how we feel. Repression has become quite acceptable when applied to emotions. With that in mind, you can set the tone for your reader by addressing the emotional and related physiological responses a character may have to a situation in the narrative or the inner monologue, writing in such a way that it is clear the character is aware of the reaction, but those they are sharing the scene with are not. For example:

> Carl smiled. "You'll do it. You have no choice."
> Tammy stared at him a moment. "No, I don't think so."
> Without another word, she turned and walked away.

There really aren't any emotions in this exchange. A smile is an action that could have many different emotional motivators. This is a statement of facts and actions with no clues about what the characters are feeling or how the reader should feel about them. Let's give it another go:

> Carl smirked. "You'll do it. You have no choice."
> Tammy felt a sharp jab deep in her gut, brutal and cold. Swallowing a gasp, she locked down her expression, refusing to let her features betray her as he just had. "No, I don't think so," she answered, her tone deceptively calm. Despite the cold tinges running the length of her body, threatening to grow into uncontrollable shudders, she silently turned and walked away, holding her heartache deep inside until she reached the privacy of her room.

Thanks to Tammy's internalized responses, we know how to react to the scene, and we also know that Carl is not aware of the emotion he has inspired in her. Maybe he suspects, or maybe he assumes, but he doesn't know, which sets the tone for the encounter and the relationship between these two characters.

Can't you just hear the reader asking, *What's the deal? Where is this going?* People respond to emotion. True… in their own way, colored by their own experiences, so you can't really predict what reaction the reader will have absolutely, but there are some universals that you can be reasonably sure will resonate with the reader, particularly the physiological responses to emotion, if not what inspires said emotions.

Don't be afraid to get into the character's head — and heart — and give the reader a peek.

Unconscious Signifiers

In fiction, characters are not the only ones with emotions. Sometimes writers need to set a scene. They need to build a tone that will culminate somewhere down the line. Because of this, we need to be aware of the emotional impact of words and descriptions that motivate responses, rather than just describing them. Mostly this deals with building some sort of tension or mood in a scene that puts the reader in the right mindset or emotional state for the pending action.

For example, a character moving from one place to another can be a simple statement of fact, an action completed, and nothing more, such as:

> Chrissy stood in the doorway. Anthony moved across the room.

Or an act can be a part of the emotional climate:

> Chrissy stood in the doorway, her face pale and her dress torn. Frowning, Anthony hurried across the room.

This is a simple adjustment that layers the detail and implies the emotion, rather than putting it right out there. The reader — drawing on their own inherent responses — has to interpret the actions and events based on the cues you provide and the context surrounding them. Not only does that draw the reader in and help provide them with the "why" behind the "what," but it also further immerses them into the story, connecting them to it almost without them realizing it.

The Roles of Emotions

Emotions are a powerful tool in the writer's toolbox, adding depth and impact to any prose, particularly if properly utilized. Keep in mind that there are subtly different roles that feelings can play in a story.

Communicate – emotions and how characters react to them tell the reader and other characters about their personality, character, and motivation.

Relate – emotions provide—with hope—common ground and a basis for understanding.

Affect – emotions draw a response from others, sometimes predictable, sometimes not, often changing the course of actions.

Manipulate – emotions, in the wrong hands, can be tools or weapons, putting pressure on characters to change their stance or act against their nature.

Summing Up

As both readers and individuals, we are often left wondering. That's frustrating in life. In fiction, it is extremely dissatisfying. Let's assume we don't have much choice about life; the book, however, we can put down and forget it ever existed.

You need to remember that the reader isn't the one the character is trying to hide from, so keep that in mind as you are writing. Share with the reader, give them a glimpse of what's going on inside. They will love (or hate) your characters for it even more. But most important of all, they will *care*.

If you leave too much for the reader to infer or figure out on their own, you relinquish way too much control over your story. Tug here, jerk there… guide them through the world you have created and inspire them to see it from your perspective, through your emotional filters, or you never know what they will get out of the story… if they even finish it.

You Got Your Anachronism in My Period Piece!

Words are funny things. You think you know what they mean… and then bam! A colloquialism sneaks up and bites you… well, you get the idea.

Language is like a secret code. The same word can mean ten different things to ten different people. And you want to know what makes it worse? They change. Language is not static; it is fluid. Tell a man from the eighteenth century that he looks gay, and he might smile and nod in agreement. Tell a man that today and watch out. He's likely to punch you. And it isn't just time that changes words. They can have different connotations from region to region and across social classes.

For instance, take the word "fag;" did you know it has three different meanings?

- It is a derogatory term for a homosexual or an insult to any male.

- In England and most of the British Commonwealth, it is a slang term for a cigarette.

- It is a verb meaning 'to tire.'

Can you see how using this word in any of its contexts could confuse some portion of the world population?

If you can master the trick of this linguistic metamorphosis, you can write anything from homage to Shakespeare to a riff on Tennessee Williams just by choosing your words wisely.

It isn't easy, and you might think it doesn't really matter—say if you write fantasy, or mainstream, rather than historical or period fiction. But you know, no matter what you write, if you use the wrong word or phrase or use the right one in the wrong context, you are going to yank that reader right out of your story quicker than you can blink.

Your job as a writer is to be aware of how your words might be taken, of the tone they are setting. For example, I'm currently writing a Victorian steampunk tale, and I've chosen very formal language to convey that era:

> The gentleman stared at her with shock and affront clearly visible in his gaze, if not his expression, but he did not argue and went to do as she bid. Clara allowed him a slight, encouraging smile before he looked away. That smile quite disappeared as she turned to the inventor upon whom she bestowed her patronage.

Words like affront, bid, bestowed, and patronage are not commonly used today, at least not in everyday conversation, but you can see how they have set a formal tone to this piece. Now, look at the same passage with more modern language:

> The man stared at her with shock and outrage heating his gaze, though his expression was blank. Yet he didn't argue as he went to do as she asked. Clara allowed him a slight, encouraging smile before he looked away. That smile disappeared as she turned to the inventor she sponsored.

From the second paragraph, you would never know that this is a period piece though it conveys the same information.

Of course, most words are just words with no particular tie to a timeframe, but once in a while, something will slip in without you even realizing it, such as calling a pretty girl a babe or mentioning penicillin when your story is set before 1928. Some of that can be combated with research. As for language, try reading a sampling of things actually written in the time period you want to replicate or visit the region where you are setting your work if it is a modern piece. This will let you pick up on phrases and slang peculiar to that area.

Now, most of us are not going to pull out the dictionary every time we type a word to make sure it was in usage at the proper time or that it doesn't have some embarrassing alter-meaning that can't be distinguished from the one intended by context, but in most cases, it should be evident if you read your work aloud if something among the wording sounds off. You can also enlist a friend or two to read through and point out anything that made them stumble while reading.

And remember, watch your language... after all, you might not be saying what you meant to.

Building with Allusion

If there is one defining characteristic of the human race, it is the overwhelming need to know *why*. *Why does the sun rise each day? What makes a rainbow appear? What causes the thunder in the heavens?*

Let's face it, as a race, we have much in common with a two-year-old.

And much like that self-same two-year-old, we have a history of making up a reason to soothe our soul if one is not readily understandable. Just look at the parallels throughout the civilizations of the world. In each of them, there is a myth or legend dealing with those questions above, as well as all the other at-one-time unfathomable occurrences both in nature and human experience.

This is the second defining characteristic of the human race: creativity. Now, imagine the two paired together…

As writers, particularly of speculative fiction, old answers — myths and legends — can add depth and meaning to our writing as we present our readers with new questions. Whether it is a key part of the plot or a hidden significance in the details, literary allusion is like the spice in a good sauce, not always obvious, but definitely enriching. No matter what myth cycle or legend you borrow from, chances are at least a percentage of your readership will be familiar with the original.

I believe very much in borrowing such references, not only because it keeps them alive, but because they make for great fiction. Let's take a look at how…

Names

Borrowing names — or even whole characters — from mythology serves several purposes for you, the writer. First, it makes the reader feel good when they recognize the reference, like they got the in-joke. Second, it helps both you and the reader define the characteristics at play. For instance, if you name a character Lucifer, that name comes with some automatic connotations based on the biblical reference. This tells the reader right away what they should expect, or gives you as the writer a foil to work against if your purpose is to overturn those preconceived notions. And third, it can be used to foreshadow events to come. For instance, in my science fiction story "Building Blocks" (*Barbarians at the Jumpgate*, Padwolf Publishing; 2010), I named a ship the *Cortez*. It was an exploratory vessel that unknowingly caused harm to a life form the crew was not even aware of until it started to fight back. In another story, "Carbon Copy" (*Space Pirates*, Flying Pen Press; 2007), I named a state-of-the-art warship the *Rommel*. In these cases, both historical references, but still relevant.

Ultimately, my point is mythology (or history) is full of names: heroes, villains, creatures, all of them can help build a character, defining for the writer — if no one else — what that character should be like, or provide a focal point from which your story can grow.

Plots

There is a popular opinion that there are no new stories, only new tellings. That doesn't have to be a bad thing. By using an established legend or myth as the foundation of your story, you have a better understanding of the steps that need to take place, and that gives you the freedom to play along the way, rather than having to figure out where you're going next. For example, my first novel, *Yesterday's Dreams*, takes aspects of Celtic mythology and actually weaves them into the plot. This is how it happened: I named my antagonist Olcas — which is Gaelic for evil — and while researching Irish mythology, I discovered there actually *was* an Olcas in legend. He and his family terrorized ancient Ireland until they were brought down and destroyed by the Sidhe (Irish elves). By incorporating these details into my novel, I now had a concrete goal for my bad guy (other than just being the bad guy). He wanted revenge, he wanted to triumph over those that had destroyed his family, and he wanted power like he had had before. And what was more… he had two brothers who wanted the same thing, which meant I had much more story to tell and more factions to play with than those I had when I started out. Two other books worth, in fact!

Another plot use for myths and legends is as a template, not using the actual details of the myth but using the familiar landmarks to tell a different story. In fact, mimicking existing myths with legends of your own is a great way to ease a reader into a universe of your own creation.

Characters

Both legends and myths have archetypes or tropes that most of us recognize… the white knight, the wicked witch, the damsel in distress, and the learned wizard, to mention some of the most familiar. Now, you can call them whatever you want, but the reader will still recognize them for what they are and anticipate what is to come, and understand what their role will be in the story.

Again, not necessarily a bad thing.

Whether it is a primary character (like the above-mentioned Olcas) or a background character, drawing from mythology awakens an echo in the reader's subconscious or even outright recognition. That makes the writer's job easier and frees up your mental muscle for those things you do have to figure out on your own. It also gives you room to play. For instance, my novel *The Halfing's Court* is about biker faeries. Most people don't realize that the first biker gangs were started by retired Air Force personnel. In the Air Force, if something went wrong with the plane, it was gremlins; when they became bikers, that translated. Anything that went wrong with the bike was blamed on *road* gremlins. I was able to incorporate and expand on that myth. Now, most people have some vague understanding of what a gremlin is, and probably some concept of what they look like, but where I got to play was in describing one tailored to the road. Mythology is full of descriptions of legendary beings that mimic their surroundings… I capitalized on that… and had a lot of fun! Here is my description of a road gremlin:

> "As the biker rode away down the center of the road, the puddle bubbled and seethed. Up from its shallow depth popped an odd, tiny creature, clutching at its ears. "Smear doesn't like the faerie-man. Not at all. Or his bloody little shrill bell. Smear wants to grind his face, crush the bell." Crouched upon the road, he slammed his thick, meaty fists against the asphalt. Microfissures formed: the conception of a pothole.
>
> He was joined by another, and then another, crawling up through the fissures, expanding them, until the puddle was gone. Standing in its place was a troupe of inch-high gremlins, identical in every way: Skin as grey as asphalt, with an oily, rainbow shimmer. Hair long and thick and spiny, like a porcupine mated with a box of nails. A thick white line ran down the center of their faces, like war paint, and along their arms were thick black squiggles. Like tats or tribal markings, only with the dull gleam of tar snakes. Each finger was like a spike, reminiscent of those found at toll booths and security gates, only jointed. The minuscule troupe rumbled and grumbled as they watched the bike speed away."

As you can see, I used physical characteristics of the road, combined with the slang bikers use, to take the concept of a road gremlin and not only make it my own but did so in a way that the reader can identify with and appreciate.

Summing Up

Literary allusion — be it mythology, history, or current events — is an invaluable tool for enriching your fiction, and not just that of the speculative type. Mythology and legend are a fundamental part of who we are… use that, stir up echoes in the mind that make the reader wonder, that put them in awe, draw them into your telling of a timeless story. This is a tool of such diversity. Grab it with both hands, and have some fun!

Doing Battle with The Anti-Muse

Writer's Block is a myth, right? Sad to say, it is not.

Sometimes things go beyond Writer's Block.

I went through a period in my life where I could not write. I knew what I needed to write. Basically, what needed to happen. They were all established characters. And yet, the story refused to be told.

It was very demoralizing. In trying to push my way past, I aggravated the situation by failing time and again.

Yes… I've done this. I literally owed fans a novella. Just a novella! Not even a full book. It took me five years to complete it. Part of the problem was that the novella was a spin-off from a trilogy. Another part of the problem was the novella was the start of a new series. The scope of the project boggled me.

How much does the reader need to know? What don't they? Whatever that ends up being, how do I convey the back story without bogging down the tale in infodumps?

It wasn't an easy prospect, this novella. And yet, I was committed. Not that the fans hadn't given up hope after a certain point. There are only so many times they can hear, 'Life happens, but I'm over it. I've got this now… '

Five times I had false starts. How do you get past that?

Here are some tips.

Know Your Material

If you are writing based on existing material, review that material first. Reread everything relevant and note those elements that could potentially relate to the new content you are writing. This is both for continuity, and so you know what to include, not just for those familiar with the universe, but for those who are encountering it for the first time. You don't want to retell the existing books, but if the storyline is related, a certain amount of back story will need to be included in some way for your current story to make sense.

Decide What You Need To Write

Sounds obvious, right? Not so easy, not so straightforward. For one thing, not everyone works with an outline. For another, if you knew what you needed to write, you'd just do it... right? Oh, if only!

I am a 'pantser.' This means I write without an outline. I get an idea and run with it until I get another idea. Kind of like a scavenger hunt where my prize is the story. Or maybe a hedge maze! I do a LOT of wandering around. It works for me. But I still need an idea of the story I want or need to tell.

In the case of *Eternal Wanderings* (the novella I owed everyone), I knew precisely the tale I was going to tell. I'd even written a good piece of it. But it was dry and boring and angsty. My character, Kara O'Keefe, had moved well past angsty at this point. With each of my many false starts, I got a better idea of what needed to be on the page and what did not. I read and reread what I managed to get down and identified where the gaps were and what I was missing. Everything took place within the confines of a Romani caravan, so I ended up with a lot of repetition, a lot of the same feel. That needed to be switched up.

I also ended up with many tense scenes, all with the same emotional tone and dwelling too much on past events. Some of that was needed, but not only does a good story require contrasting tones, but I also needed to keep in mind character growth. Without that, you don't have much of a story. Static is not interesting.

So, whether you outline or not, think about the story you want to tell and consider how to make it well-rounded. Know the points you don't want to leave out and consider which ones you do.

Research Until You Drop

When you write, you are creating a world. Sometimes it is completely made up. Sometimes it is a mirror of the world we live in. In either case, it should be clearly drawn and explored for the reader. Not necessarily every extraneous detail, but elements relevant to the character's experience and the story you are telling. For me, that meant I needed to learn what a Romani caravan looks like, how the people dress, something of their outlook on life. What is acceptable. What is *not*. For me, the internet provided pretty much all I needed to fill in those details.

Not writing a real-world analog? That just means you need to explore your world in detail, so you reveal that world to your reader. Understand the how and the why of things, research how things work, and what different types of environments or cultures are like and what they produce so your made-up world can follow guidelines that will make sense to the reader.

Try Something Else

Is it everything, or just one thing that you cannot write? Has your current project become an albatross? Take a break. Try writing something just for the heck of it. Something that doesn't matter nearly so much as the one hanging over your head. And if that doesn't work…

Be At Peace

If you can't write, you can't write. Accept that.

Now, I'm not saying that you shouldn't try. Sit down, give it a go. But don't follow your doubts down a rabbit hole if today isn't that day. When I was supposed to be writing *Eternal Wanderings,* I second-guessed everything I had on the page and just could not see which direction I should go. I was convinced everything I wrote was crap, and I was no longer a storyteller. My mind no longer generated random ideas, and my thumb drive was full of isolated files where I pulled stuff out of the manuscript and just couldn't throw it away.

Then... one day... five years later! I woke up with my mind buzzing and a new direction to go in. I wrote or rewrote a third of the story on that day. Within two weeks, I was done. It was nothing I could predict. The stresses of life hadn't gone away. New things kept happening. There were still life problems I had (and need) to sort out. But I had stopped second-guessing myself. I had relaxed into 'when it's time.'

Sometimes it is the anxiety of needing to write that makes it impossible. Give yourself a break because agonizing over it is counterproductive.

Don't give up, but don't try to force it either.

Writing Exercises

This section is meant to complement the articles you've just read. They are exercises I have used in writers seminars over the year and have found useful. I hope you do as well. There is one exercise to a page so that you may photocopy them if you wish to complete the exercise on the page with the instructions for reference. Feel free to do so for the purpose of honing your craft.

Writing Exercise – Nonverbal Cues: All of us have been told over and over, "Show, don't Tell." Easy to say, but how do you do it? Particularly with feelings, it is easy to fall into telling. How do you show how someone feels? I'd say to pay attention to your own reactions, but most of the time, we don't even notice. So what are you to do? Just look at those around you! All of us have subconscious or conscious reactions to emotion. While everyone does react differently, there are some typical physical acts that correspond to recognizable feelings. Unfortunately, that makes them not only cliché but also potentially repetitive in fiction. In this exercise, describe three different physical cues for the listed emotions.

   Example: Anger – (Her fists clenched. His temple pulsed. She ground her teeth. He punched the wall.)

Embarrassment

Excitement

Frustration

Hatred

Despair

Confusion

Fear

Hurt

Writing Exercise – Nonverbal Cues: People and emotions are both complex. Sometimes we feel more than one thing at once. Sometimes certain reactions represent different feelings for each person. We can get an idea of which is appropriate by context, but knowing what is potentially conveyed is important, so you know when you need to make it clearer. For this exercise, write down all the different feelings you can think of that could apply to the different physical cues (For this, I am counting anything that would complete the sentence "I feel," which could be an emotional or physical feeling).

Example: Bright eyes. Sorrow, Excitement, Pain, Joy

Clenched jaw/hands

A twitch/tic

Taut muscles

A scream

Looking away

Tears

A smile

A head toss

A clap

Writing Exercise – Description: as writers, we need to be observant. Capturing a person, object, or scene with just a few lines of description can be difficult, but we are called on to do it all the time, introducing a reader to a world or character in small glimpses at a time. In teams, go to a public location and select a person to observe for about five or ten minutes. You should both select the same subject. If it is a person, do not stare or otherwise make them uncomfortable, be discreet. When you are done observing, leave the area and go somewhere you can write. It doesn't matter where, as long as you leave the vicinity of your subject. You and your partner both write down a description of what you observed. When done, compare to see the differences of what you picked up on. Be sure to note physical characteristics, actions, and expressions, where applicable. This can be done individually as well, but doing it as a team exercise allows you to see the differences in perspective and how people can see the same thing at the same time but see it differently.)

Writing Exercise – Character Building. When writing a story or a novel, it is important to know your characters. What they look like, what drives them, and what experiences in their past impact how they act now. Some characters will only be seen in passing; others will be the foundation of your story. Waiting to discover who they are as you write can lead to pitfalls and inconsistencies later... or extra work re-writing as you have to go back and clean up the details. Using the description you came up with in the previous exercise, develop a character filling in the points provided.

Name:
Hair color:
Eye color:
Build:

Goal:

Strength:

Flaw:

Unique identifying feature:

Defining personal history:

Getting Down to Business

Putting On Your Virtual Game Face

(Originally published in Infinite Horizons Issue 1, by Avalon Games)

The internet is amazing! Absolutely amazing! In the last twenty-five years (give or take), it has totally transformed most of our lives, including how we do business. It has simplified the way we communicate, the way we pay bills and buy goods — not to mention the astounding plethora of ways in which we can now be taken advantage of — and, as writers, it has in many cases completely revamped how we submit our work for publication.

Like I said… Amazing!

And as easy as it has become to submit our work; it has become correspondingly easy for that work to be rejected.

So, why have I felt compelled to write about this? Well, as some of you might know, I am also an editor.

You know what that means?

I see up close and personal many of the mistakes individuals make when submitting electronically.

I also happen to know that most editors and publishers receive so many submissions on a daily basis that they *look* for reasons to reject them. Heck, they look for reasons to not even read them, or to stop reading them if they have indeed started.

Don't get bent out of shape about that. It's the only way they can get through the piles of submissions in anything resembling a timely manner, and if you have not put forth your best face in the cover letter or the first few paragraphs of your work, they are going to presume you haven't in the rest of it either, automatically relegating you to the dreck pile whether that descriptive applies or not.

So, that brings me to the problem with email. It fosters a sense of informality. That's fine when you are chatting up your new internet love or sending a letter to your mom, but when you are doing business, it's important to remember that while the medium has changed, the proper conventions have not. Sadly, this does not seem to be as common knowledge as I would expect.

(Time to get out the *Miss Manners* books, folks.)

If you haven't gathered yet, this is something of a pet peeve with me. Nothing bothers me more than someone sending me a query or submission that is informal to a fault or downright unprofessional. It is even worse when it is someone I know or have worked with previously. Frankly, it shows a lack of respect, and if I as an editor am to do my job, it is vital that there be an exchange of respect.

First Contact

In most cases, the first time you interact with an editor will be via a letter, be it print or electronic. That makes it that much more important to make the right impression. With that in mind, let's take a look at the proper elements of a formal letter and see how they need to be adapted for the electronic medium:

Date – Here is our first difference; in written letters, the date comes first at the top of the page, and that must be added. With email, the date is part of an automatic timestamp, so this is a no brainer... you couldn't get it wrong if you tried... well... unless you happen to be submitting before a submission period has opened or after it has closed, but that is a topic for yet another article, isn't it? Anyway...

Address – well, that one is likewise simple enough, whether print or electronic, mail must include information on where it is to be delivered. If this information is not correct, your communication will not reach the individual it is intended for. With that in mind, always confirm you have the address correct. With print mail, sometimes a simple error in the address will not matter as the post office goes to some extreme effort to make sure mail gets where it is intended to go, practicing some amount of detective work when an address is clearly incorrect or in part illegible, or returning the mail to the sender if delivery is not possible. With electronic mail, errors are of much more concern. There are three possible outcomes:

- You will get an error message that says your mail cannot be sent.

- You will get a Mailer Daemon message saying your mail cannot be delivered.

- Your mail will be delivered, but to an individual other than the one it was intended for. If you are very lucky, they will be kind enough to email you to inform you of your mistake; if you are just a little lucky, all they will do is delete it, but you will never know it has not gone where it is supposed to; if the luck gods completely frown upon you, this unknown individual will use your content for their own gain.

So… be sure to confirm the address to ensure it is both typed correctly and the proper address to send your material to.

Subject – Unlike a personal or informal letter, business letters sometimes contain a subject line, making them much like emails today. In the case of submissions, it would likely be something like the following:

- RE: Story Submission – <Insert Title>, or

- RE: Story Proposal – <Insert Title>, or

- RE: Query – Story Submission – <Insert Title>

You get the idea. Again, this is yet another parallel between print and electronic mail. It is also one of those areas where professionalism often breaks down. When you are just connecting with friends or family, the subject line and its formatting doesn't really matter. In fact, there are times when many of us haven't even bothered to include one. Not a big deal, right?

Mostly, unless we are talking about business.

When communicating by email, always... *always* include a subject line. Make sure it is professional, clear, and spelled correctly. Do not get clever. Do not be sloppy. Do not be informal. Depending on the content of your communication, something similar to the above examples would be appropriate, unless, of course, the venue you are mailing to has provided specific guidelines regarding what the subject line should be. Always check to confirm, as this is a common practice among the major magazines and publishers that accept online submissions. Ultimately, your subject line should be relevant, brief, and professional when dealing with business matters. (In case I have somehow been unclear in this, that includes all initial communications between prospective authors and any publishers, agents, or editors you may contact regarding your work; the only time you should be informal is if the professional you are contacting has initiated and/or encouraged that tone themselves.)

Greeting – It is important to acknowledge who you are emailing. It shows you have manners, and it also confirms the email went where it was intended to go. In some cases, you will know who that is by name, sometimes you will not. Here are some ways to deal with the matter:

- **To Whom It May Concern –** This is perhaps a bit dated but acceptable to use when you do not have the name of the individual that will be receiving your submission.

- **Dear Sir or Madam –** again, this may be considered dated, but a reasonable greeting for situations where you don't have a specific name, or for situations where you have a name but the gender of the individual is not readily identifiable.

- **Dear Mr. or Ms. <Insert Last Name> –** In an initial contact where you have a person's name, and that name is gender-specific, it is best to opt for a more formal approach unless and until that individual indicates otherwise. In the case of women's names, always preface with the suffix Ms., unless you know their marital status. You want to be formal initially because you want to establish your professionalism and because it is a sign of respect.

- **Dear <Insert First Name>** – This form of address is recommended in only three instances: when you have a previous relationship with the individual; when the individual makes it clear you may be familiar by closing an email with their first name only; when the individual specifically requests that you use their first name. Again, this comes down to professionalism and respect.

- **Name Only** – Some feel the use of "Dear" as a greeting is dated and somewhat uncomfortably personal, resulting in its omission in many communications. Each person will have their own feeling on the matter, but apart from using the word "Dear," the two previous bullet points should come into play in this regard.

- **Omitting the Greeting** – as I mentioned earlier, the internet fosters a sense of informality. Thus, the trend has developed of omitting a greeting altogether, with the assumption that email addresses are so specific to an individual that a greeting is not needed. It is assumed that the mail is clearly for that individual. That is your call, but keep in mind that your level of professionalism will sometimes be the deciding factor in the outcome of a query. In those instances, the recipient's view on the matter will be the deciding factor, not your own. My advice is to always err on the side of being more formal; it is much less likely to reflect poorly upon you as a professional. This, of course, applies to initial communications only, as you should be able to use your own judgment after that point to determine what is appropriate based on the other individual's responses.

Content – in publishing—as with most businesses—people generally have more work than they do time. With that in mind, the body of your email should be brief, clear, and professional. Before you email a query or a submission, always be sure to check the publisher, agent, or editor's website for any specific guidelines that might apply to your situation. They will often list exactly what they want in a cover letter (if they want one at all), what additional information they might need, and how they would like to receive it. And for goodness sake, make sure you spelled everything correctly and used good grammar! They aren't going to have much confidence in your submission if you can't show them you can write a basic letter properly.

To give you an idea of what they look for:

- **Information on your story (or proposed story):** title, word count or anticipated word count, genre, and if it is part of a planned series.

- **Information on you:** your name, contact information, the highlights of any pertinent publishing history, and any major awards you may have received.

- **Proposals/Synopses:** Some publishers don't want to receive a full manuscript. They ask for the first three chapters, or sometimes just a proposal and a marketing plan (that's a whole other article's worth of information, so don't even ask… yet). When a proposal is requested, they want basically a book report on exactly what happens, not every single detail—because, you know, that would be, like, sending them the whole book—but the key events. This is not the time to be coy and mysterious; they want to know what makes your book interesting and unique, they do not want hints and implications. Check the internet and you will find plenty of resources telling you how to write an effective proposal.

Conclusion – This is your choice, but I always like to end on a gracious note. Thank them for giving them your attention before you sign off.

Closing – Yet again, another convention that may seem out-dated, but traditionally all letters included a polite sign-off before the name of the person writing the letter. This is still a good practice. Some of the more common and applicable ones are: Sincerely, Best regards, and Thank you. Don't get fancy, don't be quirky. It is more likely to reflect poorly on you than anything else. The cover letter should inform, not distract.

Signature – Or, in the case of the internet, eSignature. This should be your full name, first and last. There are several reasons for this. First off, it is both polite and professional; second, in all likelihood, the person receiving this does not know you personally; and lastly, particularly with submissions, there is a very good chance that your cover letter may become disassociated with your actual manuscript. All of that makes it important that someone looking at one or the other can identify that they are related, and you can't bank on your title being unique and distinctive.

A second note on this, you should use your legal name on a cover letter, rather than a pen name, as that is what the publisher will use for contracts or checks, should you be fortunate enough to reach that stage. If you write under a pen name, however, mention that in your cover letter. (If nothing else, it will help them verify which letter goes with which manuscript when things get invariably jumbled.)

Example: Submission Letter
To: editor@publisher.com
RE: Submission – Yesterday's Dreams

Dear Sir or Madam,
Attached, please find my novel, Yesterday's Dreams, an urban fantasy based on Irish Mythology. The manuscript is approximately 119,000 words long.
While this is my first novel, my short stories have appeared in Tales of the Talisman Magazine and the award-winning Defending the Future anthology series. I am also the senior editor of the award-winning Bad-Ass

Faeries anthology series. To find out more about my work, please visit www.sidhenadaire.com.

Thank you in advance for your time and consideration; I look forward to hearing back from you.

Best Regards,

Danielle McPhail (writing as Danielle Ackley-McPhail)

Example: Query Letter
To: agent@getmebucks.com
RE: Query – Yesterday's Dreams

Dear Sir,

My name is Danielle Ackley-McPhail, and I am looking for representation for my novel, Yesterday's Dreams, an urban fantasy based on Irish Mythology. This is the first in a proposed three-book series.

In the novel, Kara O'Keefe, a first-generation Irish-American with elven blood, must pawn her cherished heirloom violin to save her family from eviction. To that end, she takes it to the pawnshop, Yesterday's Dreams, where the pawnbroker, Maggie McCormick, is actually one of the Celtic Sidhe sworn to protect the O'Keefe clan. This chain of events brings Kara and her magical potential to the attention of Olcas, an ancient and evil foe of the Sidhe. Unwittingly caught between the two forces, Kara struggles with the changing boundaries of her world while fighting to remain free.

The novel is complete, at approximately 119,000 words. May I send it to you for your consideration?

Thank you and best regards,

Danielle Ackley-McPhail
www.sidhenadaire.com

Following Up

It is very tempting, particularly with the ease of internet communications, to pester someone you have sent your work to for consideration. Resist. Hard. Editors are overworked, short on time, and often short on patience. If you make a nuisance of yourself, there is a good chance it will have the opposite of the desired effect. Most publishers' websites give you an idea of the response time you can expect. Look for that, mark it on your calendar, create a reminder in Outlook or whatever calendar program you have on your computer, and whatever you do, do not email the editor about your submission until after that date. It is okay to follow up, but not to pester.

When you send a submission directly to an individual, they will send you an acknowledgment email. Respond to that with your thanks, and then forget about the whole thing for a while until sufficient time has passed to make a follow-up reasonable.

Example: Follow-Up Letter

To: editor@hurryupandwaitpub.com
RE: Submission – Yesterday's Dreams

July 6, 2011

Dear Editor,

I submitted the above novel to you for consideration on January 6, 2011. It has been six months, and per your website, I am following up to ask if you have had a chance to review the manuscript.

I await your decision.

My best,

Danielle Ackley-McPhail

Dealing With Rejection

I guarantee you that you will receive a rejection in response to a query or submission at some point. In fact, there is an excellent chance you will receive many; more, in fact, than you will receive acceptances or contracts, if you are like most of us. (Let's face it, if it were otherwise, you wouldn't be reading this book!) It is very important for your potential career that you never, *ever* respond to a rejection letter, unless it is to thank them for their time and the opportunity to submit.

- Do not rail at them for not seeing the brilliance of your work.

- Do not threaten them.

- Do not plead or pester.

- Do not demand to know why.

All of the above will serve but one purpose: to lock you into the publisher/agent/editor's memory as, at best, a difficult person to work with and not worth the hassle; at worst, a crackpot worthy of a restraining order. I cannot tell you how many stories I have heard about hopeful authors that have damaged their chances by such unprofessional behavior.

However, if you do choose to respond to the rejection politely and professionally, you will likely stand out in the editor's memory, which may serve you well in the future, should you submit other stories to the same venue.

Example: Rejection Acknowledgement Letter

To: thatdamnededitor@publisher.com
RE: RE: Your Submission

Dear Editor,

Thank you for informing me of your decision. I am sorry the story did not meet your needs, but I appreciate your feedback and look forward to future opportunities to submit.

My best,

Danielle Ackley-McPhail

Summing Up

There is a lot of competition in the publishing industry. A lot of those people don't know what they are doing. Not saying that to be mean. It's just a fact. Heck, there have certainly been times when I've been out of my element, so I definitely know of which I speak, as they say. Your job, should you choose to acknowledge it, is to distinguish yourself from those who haven't got a clue. Clearly, you have already displayed initiative in that regard.

Think of it this way: letters — even by email — are a time-delayed conversation. You aren't there to clarify. You aren't there to respond to questions. That means you have to be clear the first time. And wait... it gets better...

When dealing with editors, it's more like speed-dating... with someone whose calendar is already booked. That means you have to do all the above in sixty seconds or less. You want to make a good impression, you want to hook their interest, you want to be asked out on a date, in a manner of speaking. That means you get to be on your best behavior, or you find some other goal to pursue.

So... *be* polite... *be* professional... and eventually, there's a better chance you will *be* an author.

The Importance of Respect

This should seem obvious. Professionals doing business show respect. This is from both sides of the table. So many times, I see evidence of disrespect. Sometimes overt, sometimes subtle and unrealized.

If you wish to be taken seriously as an author or publishing professional, always remain respectful.

Guidelines Exist for a Reason

One of the biggest ways I feel disrespected as a professional is when I receive an unprofessional manuscript. This can take many forms, from non-standard formatting to missing information. Take the time to check a publisher's website for submission guidelines. How they want things sent, which information they want included, and how they would like it to appear on the page. There are reasons for all of these. You may not know or understand, but respect that they serve a purpose.

What? You say there were no guidelines? Fair enough, but standard guidelines do exist. Look for them. It shows that you care enough to be professional.

Something I see quite often, which is my personal pet peeve, is when an author sends in a manuscript without the basic information at the top of the page. Maybe they have left off their address, maybe they have left off their name, maybe all of that. There have been times when they have even left off the title of the work. There are several problems with this. First, even if you have provided the missing information in your communication, the person receiving the file may not have access to the original file. What does that mean for you? Unless they are extremely forgiving, it means you have blown your chance. Most publishing professionals don't have the time or inclination to track down missing information, and if they don't know who to send a contract to or where to send it, you're never getting to the stage where they don't know where to send the check.

For me, every manuscript I send out has the basic information, even when I am sending it to someone I know. Heck, even manuscripts I am writing for *myself* include the basic information. Not only is it a matter of professionalism and not forming bad habits, but who is to say the story won't be sent to someone else at a future date? Including legal name, address, email, story title, and penname on your manuscripts shows you respect the person receiving it and do not want to make their life more difficult by forcing them to request or track down the missing information… or too easy, should they simply decide to reject the piece without reading it.

What You Say and How You Say It

Communication is an important part of respect. Both in your choice of words and the effort you take to use them. Even more so is knowing when not to say a thing. Of highest importance, however, is tone. As an author, editor, and publisher, I know from experience how difficult it can be to show restraint and how important it is.

As authors, you should always be aware of your words and the impact they have. Whether you are sending in a query or responding to feedback, your comments reflect on you more than they reflect on the other person in the conversation.

Queries – be confident, but not arrogant. Always thank the person you are submitting to for their time and express that you are open to feedback. These tell the person receiving the query that you are professional.

Feedback – If the feedback is private, such as editorial, be respectful. Do not challenge, even if you do not agree. This does not mean you are obligated to accept the feedback, but discuss the elements in question and explain your disagreement. This is a matter where tone is of utmost importance. Editors invest hours of time and effort to help authors polish their work. You may not agree with everything said but find a way to address the issues pointed out to you, rather than question their need, to begin with. Most editors are open to discussion and will not push a point unless it is major. You always have the option to withdraw, but it is not wise to be arrogant or combative if you wish to work in the industry. At the least, you will have blacklisted yourself with that editor or publishing house; at the worst, you will have blacklisted yourself with anyone that editor knows, should they share their experience.

If the feedback is public, such as a negative review or blog, be silent. You can say little to nothing in response to such things that will not reflect more poorly on yourself as a public figure than the original feedback by itself. Responding to such things can easily escalate and become even more visible than if you left it alone.

Public forums – Whether online or in person, you may have occasion to interact with your fan base or potential fan base. Never forget that you are a public figure, a celebrity to those who aspire to what you have achieved. Fans and potential fans deserve respect from you just as much as editors and publishing professionals do. They are the ones to lift you to whatever level of success you achieve. Connect with your fans, and you have loyalty beyond imagine; disrespect them, and they will let the world know.

Respect Yourself

When you are a public figure of any kind, there is no such thing as private. What you say or do in your downtime has the potential to affect your public persona. Does this mean your life is no longer your own? Not really. But it is possible that your private life will become a matter for public discussion. Whether an indiscretion or a harsh altercation, a political view or a crazy-ass stunt. Public opinion can be harsh, even about things that are none of their business… what am I saying, especially about things that are none of their business. Not only can this impact you with your fans, but it can also impact you with publishers who may not wish to be associated with some aspect of your past. Such things make them question what you might potentially do or say in the future.

Give 'Em What They Want!
Why Formatting Is Important

(Originally published in The Writer's Toolbox, Allegory Magazine)

Telling a great story is not enough.

Having the best grammar is not enough.

Hitting the perfect market trend is not enough.

Nothing is enough if the editor in question is not willing to read your manuscript.

The Truth about Submissions

Psst! I have a secret for you… well, not really a secret, unless you are *really* new at this, but anyway… here it goes:

Editors *look* for reasons NOT to read your manuscript.

(ooh… I can just hear a lot of minions going, "Wha?!")

Sorry, it's true; I'm not making it up.

See, the reality is thousands and thousands of people want to be authors. Even though only a small portion of those following the dream ever reach the stage of actually submitting something, that still means that editors of all sorts have piles and piles of things they need to go through. And frankly, most of it is dreck. Editors just don't have the time or inclination to put in extra effort puzzling through a manuscript that only might be acceptable and then cleaning it up afterward. Think about it. The longer the production process takes, the longer money bleeds out instead of—with hope—flooding in.

Besides, they want to know you can follow directions, and there are very few publishers out there—book or short fiction—that do not have submission guidelines available somewhere.

Look for them. And if you don't find them, ask! You want to stand out because of the quality of your writing, not because your manuscript is an annoyance filled with stylistic errors. The best thing you can do is show that you will make extra effort to meet their requirements.

Of course, even if you don't have the publisher's submission guidelines, there are plenty of things that are standard. Let's take a look.

The Basics

Contact information. No matter who you are sending your work to or how many times you have sent them work before, you always—let me repeat that—ALWAYS include your full contact information in the upper left hand of the page. (The editor could be your brother, and you should still follow this rule, if nothing else but because it is common courtesy and shows you respect the relationship between hopeful author and potential publisher.) For me, I make sure to do this even when I am writing something I intend to publish myself. Why? Because one, who is to say I won't at some point send that story to someone else for consideration; and two, it is all too possible I could do it the wrong way when it *does* matter if I let bad habits form by not being consistent in how I set up my files.

If you aren't sure what is considered full contact information, here it goes: legal name, mailing address, email address, and optionally, phone number. I can't tell you how many times I have received manuscripts without this information. Usually from an author I've worked with before, but not always. See, we fall into a trap of informality thanks to the internet. With so many manuscripts being submitted electronically, we don't always consider that the email might become disassociated from the manuscript file, thus leaving the publisher no way to contact the author. Bad enough when what is forthcoming is a rejection. An absolute tragedy when they want to send you an acceptance. Face it... they have to know where to send the contract... or the check!

Identifiers. To simplify, I'm grouping several things under this heading, so bear with me.

Title – you would be amazed how many people neglect to put titles on their manuscripts (coincidentally enough, more than a few of them are the ones who forgot contact information as well).

Name – your pen name or your legal name, whichever one you write under. Editors like to know whose work they are reading and what should appear on a published work (should you be fortunate enough to make a sale.) The problem is that if the contact information is missing *and* there is no title or author name, the publisher has absolutely no way of cross-referencing to try and determine what story goes with which submission email (assuming they will even try).

Page Numbers – now you might be thinking, "But manuscripts are electronic. How can the pages get out of order?" Well, first, you can't assume that whoever receives the manuscript won't prefer to review a hardcopy. Second, even if they are reviewing something electronically, it is easier for them to make notes or track back if there are page numbers to reference.

Running Headers – This is the space at the top of the page (starting with page 2) where you put the story/book title, the page number, and your legal last name. This is so no pages go missing, and the editor knows what they are reading.

Author Bio – Optional, but a good thing to include, particularly if you have a few sales under your belt, but only if they are professional sales of note, not a piece of flash fiction you sold to a fanzine. What this tells the editor is that you are already established.

Besides the more practical reasons for not omitting any of the above information, consider that it is just plain sloppy and unprofessional. This isn't a matter of wanting to impress the editor. It is showing them that you are not an amateur without a clue. Professionalism will do much to smooth over any other short fallings you have in the editor's eye.

Format

Some things are just industry standard. If you are serious about becoming an author, you should learn what those are. If you are submitting somewhere that for one reason or another does not have submission guidelines, always assume they want the following formatting:

Font – Courier or Times New Roman, 12 point. These fonts are clear and easy to read, and 12 point is generally a comfortable size for most people.

Spacing (Print) – paragraphs should be first-line indented and double-spaced, with no line break between paragraphs. Some programs have an automatic indent feature. These can cause problems in the typesetting process, so, personally, I feel it is better to use a tab for your first line indent. Not sure if any publishers or editors (besides myself) express a preference on that. In either case, whichever you chose, use it consistently.
It also used to be the convention to double space after a period. This hails from the days when manuscripts had to be manually typeset. It is no longer necessary in the age of computers and digital typesetting, though many still do so simply because it was how they were originally taught.

Spacing (Online) – paragraphs should be flush left (no indent) and single-spaced, with a line break between paragraphs.

Section Breaks – when a scene changes, it is very important the transition is clearly marked. Some authors simply use a line space between the scenes. Others use either a number sign (#) or three asterisks (***), making it clear the break is intentional. It is better to use an actual character; otherwise, a scene break might not be evident if a scene break happens across a page break.

The End – Generally a good idea to close your manuscript with these words, so it is clear to the person reviewing it that nothing is missing.

Special characters/formatting – originally, when manuscripts were all submitted in hardcopy, it was not possible to implement certain formatting or characters on a typewriter. Because of this, certain conventions were developed to represent the formatting desired. As technology progressed, this changed, thanks to the advent of electronic typewriters and word processors, which had features for special formatting. This formatting issue was rendered altogether moot once computers were on the scene. However, even once we could represent format true to form, manuscripts still had to be physically typeset to create the plates used on a printing press as recently as the mid to late 20th century, and publishers held to the traditional conventions because special formatting was often easy to miss, causing errors in the typeset manuscript. Even now that most books are digitally typeset, some publishers still require these methods to mark the format. Here they are, for your writerly edification:

Bold – represented by asterisks bracketing the text to be set in bold.

Italic – represented by underlining text to be set in italics.

Underline – I am afraid I could not find a reference to how this was represented originally (before the age of computers), particularly given that underlining was used to indicate italics. I can only presume that is because it was and/or is exceedingly rare for underlined text to appear in books. (That, or I'm just not hitting the right search phrase that would give me the information I'm looking for.)

Emdash – represented as two hyphens. In this time of computers, most programs automatically convert the double hyphen to an emdash. Depending on the publisher's preferred style, they will have a space before and after the emdash " – " or " – " in the finished book.

Ellipsis – depending on the publisher's preferred style, these can be represented in multiple ways:

- Three periods in a row with no spaces before, after, or in between. "… "
- Three periods in a row with a space before and after. " … "

- Three periods with one character space between each period and a space before and after. " . . . "

Quotation marks and Apostrophes – many word processing programs have a feature for smart quotes or straight quotes. (For those who don't know what I mean by smart quotes, those are the curly ones.) I have never encountered a publisher who has expressed a preference either way, but I can tell you that as an editor and a typesetter, one of my biggest pet peeves is straight quotes. And let me tell you why... Even though it is possible for me to do a simple "Find and Replace" to convert straight quotes into smart quotes, it causes several formatting problems. First off, quotation marks sometimes end up facing the wrong direction when they follow punctuation that is not a period, requiring that I go in and manually turn them around. Second, in the case of apostrophes—as opposed to single quotes—when those occur at the beginning of a word, as in the case of dialect ('em, 'twere, 'twas, etc.), the program does not recognize the convention and flips it around as if it was intended as a single quote, again requiring the typesetter to go through the entire manuscript manually correcting. These aren't so difficult to correct, but they are definitely easy to miss, thus making them a headache of the highest order when they introduce errors into an already edited manuscript.

Now, as I mentioned, even though virtually every word processing or layout program has toolbars, options, or auto-formatting features that facilitate all of the above, some publishers still request that these conventions be employed when formatting your manuscript. This is one reason why it is very important to find those submission guidelines or find out which style guide the publisher employs because that will tell you how to set things up.

Don't lose heart if you can't find this information or, for some bizarre reason, can't find someone to tell you. Most editors are more forgiving when it comes to things like italics and all that as long as you are consistent in your usage. So... if you pick a style (even if it's not the one preferred) and stick with it, you will lose fewer points than if you switch back and forth.

Matters of Style

No matter what I type here, there will be plenty of examples of publishers that do things differently from what I've covered. Sometimes that is just a product of their experience or how they were taught. Sometimes it has to do with style guides. You may or may not have heard of these; the most familiar are the *AP Style Guide, the Chicago Manual of Style,* and *Strunk and Whites*. Many of these have their roots in print journalism and are meant to unify style for consistency. Basically, they are journalists' grammar and style bibles. But their use is no longer limited to newspapers or magazines. Not only do they guide a writer in matters of style, but they also cover grammar issues that are often confused or lost in depths of time-fogged memory.

Keep it Simple!

Before the time of electronic submissions, not listening to this advice was one of the biggest mistakes beginners made. You would laugh your butts off if you had heard some of the stories I have about how some hopeful authors have submitted their manuscripts. We are talking complete bells and whistles here of the type you would expect from the ad campaign of a major corporation. Everything from fancy, scented paper to puzzle-box packaging, all of it intended to catch the eye and stand out like a psychedelic dream. Unfortunately, all that does is relegate your manuscript to the list of over-drinks stories editors tell.

Things might have changed now that most submissions are handled electronically, but it is still important for you to know that a story should be noticed for the quality of the writing, not the inventiveness or style of its presentation. If you are submitting by conventional mail, use plain white or cream bond paper and observe the formatting guidelines I reviewed above; if you are submitting electronically, don't use fancy type or try to set your manuscript as if it is a finished book; don't use colored text or insert photographs (unless they are a key point of what you are submitting, such as an academic text or how-to); and don't add any other bells and whistles you might be considering. Let me be clear: The manuscript should stand on its own merit. If the writing isn't any good, none of the flash is going to make a difference. What it *will* do is distract the editor from your work and likely cause them to reject it outright as being unprofessional.

Summing Up

You might think this article was about the technical aspects of formatting, but you would only be partially correct. What this article is truly about is respect. If you want to succeed at this dedicated hobby you've chosen to pursue (believe me, you don't want to think of it as a career... it only leads to masses of frustration), then you need to get your head in the correct mindset. You are not alone in your desire. Countless individuals want to be authors. There are considerably fewer individuals who are in a position to make that possible. Editors have to look through hundreds, even thousands of manuscripts every year. I don't think I have to tell you that they can't accept them all. You know what that means? It is your job to make *their* job as easy for them as possible. You can do that in two ways:

- Ignore what I've shared with you here and start deciding which room you are going to wallpaper with rejections first, or

- Do everything you can to make your manuscript clean and formatted to the publisher's preference so that technical issues don't distract the editor from your work's creative aspects.

Now I'm not saying if you follow all the submission guidelines your work is guaranteed to be accepted, but I am saying you stand a heck of a better chance of getting noticed.

Convention (al) Opportunities

One of the most valuable lessons a beginning author can learn about conventions is that they are as much about seeing as about being seen. Yes, you want to get yourself and your books in the public eye. Yes, you want to distinguish yourself and get started making that pen name a household name (oh... come on... just try and tell me that's not what we're all after...) But what opportunities are you overlooking in your efforts to be noticed?

Don't let yourself be blinded by your own "celebrity." Pay attention... let your creativity stew on the occasional thought not centered on your fiction. There are many opportunities out there for cross-promotional efforts if you have the vision to recognize them. You never know when you might have an untapped resource that dovetails with someone else's need.

I've had several different instances of this crop up recently that I want to share with you as examples of the potential in all things.

You've no doubt noticed that I go on about networking. What you might not have picked up on is that networking goes both ways. At a recent convention local to me, Philcon, I had this brought home to me. First, I connected with an editor who had purchased a magazine where I had a submission under consideration. Unfortunately, my story was lost in the shuffle of transition between the old guard and the new. By introducing myself to the editor in question, I made a connection that bagged me two sales in one weekend. The editor did not want me to fear I was lost in the cracks and so instructed me to send him my story directly. I was fortunate that he enjoyed it and another story I sent along with it very much, and he took both of them.

The next day at the same convention, I was approached by one of the musical guests, Jonah Knight, purveyor of modern paranormal folk. He had seen me around the conventions and noted my visibility and success in the dealer's room, as well as having been on a rather successful panel with me earlier that day and was interested in discussing the possibility of my carrying some of his CDs at events. I was cautious about this because when you are a personality rather than just a vendor, selling others' works can be difficult if you are not directly associated with the project. That brought Jonah to his second point... he was interested in compiling a soundtrack based on my novels. We pooled our resources: connections to assemble a group of musicians and artists to participate in the project, as well as enlisting the aid of various conventions in spreading the word and arranging promotional parties.

Now, not only did I get some fantastic promotions out of the arrangement, but so did everyone involved, from the conventions down to the individual performers, the publishers, and anyone else participating. And all of it started with a handful of connections made at various events over the years.

Conventions are not just places to connect with fans. They are your best opportunity to network with other professionals. Connect, support, be open. Helping others can often prove to be the best way to help yourself and your career, not because you want to get ahead, but because the friendships you make along the way expand potential in so many unexpected ways.

Now, I know not all of you have the opportunity, desire, or resources to go from convention to convention throughout the year. If you can, great; if not, don't feel like you are doomed to be left on the outside. A lot of what I have written here can also be applied to online groups and professional organizations with an online presence.

However you reach out and try to connect, remember this: don't plot, don't scheme, don't weigh everyone and everything for prospective value to you, but never shrink away from putting yourself in the path of opportunity. It can be both fun and profitable. And oy! The people you'll meet along the way!

Building Credibility

Who do you think you are?

Yeah... confrontational, maybe, but we've been over this before. There are a LOT of would-be authors out there. That means a lot of people brandishing their first-ever book expecting the world to take notice. I'm sorry, but one book does not instantly make you a success. Not saying that to belittle anyone or scoff at anyone's accomplishments (And finishing a book is a major accomplishment). Not even saying it to discourage anyone, just trying to prepare the beginners out there for the harsh reality that blindsided me.

See, I work in publishing. That means you would expect I might have had a bit more insight than everyone else going into this wacked-out industry cold. Nope... I was a total noob.

I won't go into all the ugly details, at least not in this article. But one cold, glaring point in all of my ignoble beginning actually is relevant to what I'm writing about. As mentioned, I work in publishing, and at the time my first novel came out, I was employed by one of the "Big" publishing houses. The reason this is relevant? My first book (and every other book after that one) was not with a "Big" publisher. I am very solidly a small-press author — or independent, as they now say to put a prettier face on it. Anyway, as I was going through the initial production process, needless to say, I was very excited and would share the details with my co-workers, or those that would listen, anyway.

No big deal, right?

One day my boss's boss pulled me aside to tell me he didn't want me to talk about my book. He cited it as a conflict of interest. He really meant he thought I had self-published the book and considered it an embarrassment that reflected badly on our parent company.

(Very ironic, that, considering... but I those tales aren't mine to tell.)

At that moment, I realized that I had learned about credibility and the fact that in many eyes, I didn't have any yet. I had one book with a publisher most people had never heard of before, so yeah, I got a lot of "Who do you think you are?" Here's my point: No one knew my name. Having it printed nice and big on a couple of hundred copies of my book did not instantaneously make it common knowledge (heck, having it on several thousand hasn't either... just to put it in perspective.)

Now, if your only goal is to have your name on the front cover of a published book, credibility isn't a big deal. However, if your goal is to share your writing with the world, in as many variations as your fertile mind can come up with, it's going to take a lot of work building that credibility.

How? Well... funny, you should ask...

Making A Name

One mistake that many authors — beginning or otherwise — make is promoting books.

No, you didn't read that wrong. See, by promoting *books*, the focus is directed away from the author. What you want to do is promote yourself foremost and individual titles secondary. It's called branding.

(No, it doesn't involve superheated iron.)

Visibility – Have you ever seen playbills and promotional posters plastered over a city? I encountered this a lot in New York, boarded-up buildings or construction site fences completely covered by posters, sometimes all the same one. Now, I'm not telling you that is what you should do... precisely, but it is close. I'm actually talking about doing this virtually. Go on the internet and look for interview opportunities or author databases. Make sure you are posted on every one you can find. Use that social media for something more than bitching about the weather or groaning over your relationship drama. Create a page or user id that is just for author-related posts, and every time you have some news, share it with the world. If you can increase awareness of yourself as a good author, attention to your books (existing and upcoming) will follow. That doesn't mean make everything about you alone, but when you promote something book-related, it should be (for example) "Danielle Ackley-McPhail's new book, *Eternal Wanderings*," not "*Eternal Wanderings*, by Danielle Ackley-McPhail." I'm not talking literally. This isn't about form. The book should be as important as the next great thing from *you*. If they can remember your name, they can find everything else on their own, so whatever opportunity you have to promote, always filter it through your Brand (which is you).

Have a website where you are the focus, and the books are mentioned in relation to you. Have a printable reading list so people can more easily find your work. Do author events at conventions, schools, libraries, and bookstores.

Whether virtually or in the real world, you want the readers to associate the book title with a name and the name with a face so that you become an icon, a presence, instead of just type on a front cover.

Productivity – In most cases, it isn't enough to write one book and expect to get somewhere. It's been known to happen, but it is rare. Most authors have to build up their publishing credits. It's sad, but a lot of people are cynical. Get published once and they think it could be a fluke, you could be a one-hit-wonder, or worse, you signed with a publisher who doesn't know good fiction. That doesn't mean they are right, but it does mean you have to prove them wrong. Novels take a very long time to write and publish, but if you are one of the fortunate individuals who can write both long and short fiction, you have a branding goldmine. The more credits you have to your name, the more people will take notice of you, even if they've never read your work before. What you're showing is that your writing is good enough that someone bought it. Each sale adds to your credibility because it shows that you can stick with it and people are interested in what you write. It shows dedication and reinforces the quality of your work in their minds.

Consistency – speaking of quality of work, make it the best you can produce, grammatically, literally, accurately. Don't depend on the publisher to clean things up. There is, in theory, an editor assigned to your book who is supposed to help with that, but you can't depend on their knowledge and thoroughness. Sadly, I have learned that from experience. Produce high-quality fiction — over and over again — and then sell it to reputable, established publishers, and you will build the recognition you are looking for.

Association – There are a couple of ways this applies. First off: the publishers, since I've already mentioned them. It's not enough to get published by just anyone. You need a venue known in the industry for producing your chosen genre with quality production values, good writing, and good business practices. Face it, having a story printed in a magazine that is photocopied pages folded and stapled in the middle is not the way to come across as professional.

Speaking of professional... professional organizations. Not only are these great opportunities for networking, mentoring, and inside knowledge about the market, but they also tell the world you are serious about being a writer and elevate your visibility through the company you keep and the opportunities the organization offers.

Summing Up

Want a more positive approach? Here's a better question for you... who do you want to *be*?

(Sorry, Faith Hunter and Steven King are already taken).

If you want to be a successful author (whatever success means to you), it takes effort and the ability to put yourself out there. Engage your audience directly and indirectly. Most people like to feel touched by celebrity, and authors fall into that category, no matter the level of your success. Sell them on yourself as a brand and the books will move; sell a book with your name on it, and you have to hope the reader remembers who wrote it — and that they enjoyed it — by the next time one of your books comes out.

A Genre Primer

Are you one of those that are confused by the term genre? In truth, all fiction and media can be broken down into one genre or another; it has to… that's how the bookstore knows what section to put each book in…

(Okay… maybe that wasn't the best example…)

Mostly when people classify something as "genre fiction," they are generally talking about science fiction, fantasy, horror, mystery, or romance, and if they are old enough to know about them, they'll throw pulp or western into the pile as well. Basically, genre fiction has, to most people, come to mean anything besides mainstream (drama) fiction. Another term for this is speculative fiction.

Still confused? Well… let's look at what some of these genres are:

Fantasy – this can primarily be described as any fiction that does not adhere to reality as we experience it, where magic or supernatural creatures are a significant part of the plot, theme, and setting, and things you would consider impossible are possible. The setting is generally a world other than our own, either drawn from mythology or the writer's imagination. Well-known authors in the genre are Patricia Briggs, Mercedes Lackey, Faith Hunter, J.R.R. Tolkien, and C.S. Lewis.

Science Fiction – broken down into near future, far-future, and epic, these stories often involve projections of technology, either existing or of the author's creation, as a primary part of the plot, theme, and setting. There are often themes of military conflict (where the military aspect is secondary), colonization, and exploration. Well-known authors in the genre are Isaac Asimov, Harlan Ellison, Robert Heinlein, and Arthur C. Clark.

Horror – distinguished by the macabre or frightening, this genre is often blended with elements from fantasy or science fiction, but those elements are secondary to the primary objective of scaring the shit out of the reader. Monsters, demons, psychopaths with chainsaws... that's what we're talking about here. Expect graphic violence, depravity, and extremely dark plots, themes, and settings. Well-known authors in the genre are Stephen King, Joe Hill, Jonathan Maberry, and Bram Stoker.

Romance – Happy endings, simple, sweet romances, and lately, a bit of spice, but not too much, or this rolls over into erotica. The happy endings are the key to this genre, though... without them, it's called drama. Those who read romance know that the damsel (or dude) gets the hero by the last page. There is usually inner turmoil, perhaps nefarious deeds by a rival or other calamity, but Romeo comes to the rescue, and all conflict is resolved by the time the two of them hook up at the end. Well-known authors in the genre are Danielle Steel, Nora Roberts, and Suzanne Brockmann.

Western – historic fiction that features cowboys, robbers, steam locomotives, Indians, and some dealing with gold, for the most part. Pulp adventure for those that were loathed to put up their popguns. There may or may not be a romantic interest, but it's all about the white hat against the black, whether it's set in a bygone era or more urban in nature. Well-known authors in the genre are Louis L'Amour, Zane Grey, Willa Cather, and Larry McMurtry.

Mystery – Your basic *whodunit?* where the reader is presented with... well... a mystery, suspects, and clues throughout, and all comes clear at the end (one hopes). Sometimes the mysteries are themed, such as those involving cooking or pets, and those are usually called cozy mysteries. Well-known authors in the genre are Sir Arthur Conan Doyle, Agatha Christie, and John Grisham.

Pulp/Noir – These adventure novels featured mostly gumshoe detectives and vigilante justice, but they really touched any genre. They all had the same gritty, daring-do, cheap paper, and stylized art covers. The genre is full of icons like Tarzan, The Spider, the Domino Lady, Kolchak, and Jack Hagee. Adventure, danger, guns and violence, mobsters and dames, and rogue avengers. The good guys always get beat up, but in the end, rarely get beat. Well-known authors in this genre are Ray Bradbury, Robert E. Howard, Alfred Bester, and Arthur Conan Doyle.

Subgenres

Dark fantasy – when elements of horror play a central part in the story, but not to the extreme that would classify it as horror. Well-known authors in the genre are Neil Gaiman, Karen Marie Moning, and Scott Nicholson.

Science fantasy – when there is a scientific element to the fantasy realm (or a fantasy element to the scientific world). Well-known authors in the genre are David Sherman, Larry Niven, and Piers Anthony.

Urban fantasy – Urban fantasy has the stipulation that the story, though using the same fantasy tropes, is at least in part is set in the real world, generally in a city or the suburbs of a city, rather than a country setting, though those are seen as well. Well-known authors in the genre are Charles DeLint, Holly Black, and J. K. Rowling.

Steampunk – I classify this as a subgenre because it is really, often, a blending of both fantasy and science fiction, though, in popularity, it is a force of its own. The setting is historic, most of the Victorian era. Basically, it is technology with the rules of science thrown out the window. A good example of the subgenre that everyone should be familiar with is the works of Jules Verne. It's all about the mods and gadgets. Stereotypically there are goggles, airships, detectives a la Sherlock Holmes, and steam... lots of steam. Well-known authors in the genre are Cherie Priest, Jeff VanderMeer, and Jules Verne.

Inspirational romance – The relationships are pg-13, and the story includes a religious theme or overtones. Well-known authors in the genre are Keira Knightley, Janette Oke, and Karen Kingsbury.

Historical romance – Also called regency romance as most of them are set in that era but can be in any time period though generally not current day. (Some authors do mingle now with then, but those books generally fall more under the venue of paranormal romance.) Well-known authors in the genre are Catherine Coulter, L.M. Montgomery, and Eloisa James.

Paranormal romance – At least one, if not more, of the romantic interests are a "monster," mythological creature, or ghost. The rest of the story can travel any route. Well-known authors in the genre are Sherrilyn Kenyon, Charlaine Harris, Patricia Briggs, and Jeri Smith-Ready.

Military science fiction – In this genre, the military conflict, structure, and mindset are predominant; otherwise, it is just science fiction with military elements. Well-known authors in the genre are David Weber, Jack Campbell, C. J. Cherryh, David Sherman, and John Ringo.

Thriller – I like to describe this as psychological horror, mostly about the depravity of madmen and psychopaths, and the hero saving themselves just in time. Edge-of-your-seat nail-biters, rather than behind-the-seat. Well-known authors in the genre are Lisa Gardner, Heather Graham, and James Patterson.

Erotica – Romance that is edgy and explicit. More about exploring sensuality, with "socially acceptable" boundaries pushed to the limit and beyond. Plot is generally a secondary concern. Well-known authors in the genre are Laurell K. Hamilton, Stephanie Burke, Alessia Brio, and Desiree Holt.

Media Tie-in/Shared Universe – Fiction based on popular movies, television shows, games, and occasionally comics or cartoons, or non-media-based shared world contributed to by multiple authors. There is an established universe and a "bible" that authors must adhere to when writing these types of books. Well-known authors in the genre are Keith R. A. DeCandido, Greg Cox, Will McDermott, and Alan Dean Foster.

I could keep going, you know, only I think you get the idea. But more to the point, do you understand why genre is important?

(Other than knowing where to put the book on the shelf…)

So that the reader has some idea of what is in store for them when they pick up a book. And also, to allow them to seek out other similar books to those they have enjoyed in the past… and as an excuse for fanboys and girls around the world to start up conventions so they can meet their favorite authors.

Okay… maybe not so much on that last one…

Stepping Back

Don't panic... this isn't a Dear John (or Jane) letter.

What I want to talk about now is becoming overwhelmed.

It is such an easy thing to happen to a writer or any other creative person. All of us experience it at one point or another. There are deadlines and promoting and new ideas every time you turn around... and that's just the writing stuff! We won't even talk about the family, home, and work also bidding for our times (yet.)

I know... you're nodding your head, looking a little mystified that I understand exactly what you're going through.

(Oh, come on, you know you are.)

Believe me, this dilemma is exponentially increased for those of us writers who work on the flip side of publishing, as well. Smacks of masochism, really; what, one low-paying, thankless job isn't enough?

Anyway, back to the program...

Remember to Breathe

Sounds simple, right? One of the most basic precepts of life, but have you ever been in that place where you are so overwhelmed you have to remind yourself to breathe? No? Just wait... it will happen. One of the dangers of having too many options (or obligations) is that you freeze up from time to time; you don't know what to do first, so you do nothing. The thing about nothing, though, is it fosters entropy. When you do nothing, it only exacerbates your problem.

Don't get me wrong, I'm not talking about the occasional blowing off steam or taking time for yourself or other non-writing concerns. I'm talking about the benumbed, shaking-your-head kind of nothing, you know, where your eyes glaze over, and you want to find a bed to hide under.

No? Well then, you're more fortunate than I.

Two things to do when you do reach this state:

- Take one step back and turn around. (No! Not literally!) Pick up something for fun and clear your thoughts a moment. Read a book, play a game with your family, watch a TV show. A short one! No Bingeing.

- Make a list of all the things you need to do and prioritize them. If there are deadlines, those obligations go to the top of the list, closest date first. Follow those with things that have been waiting the longest or those closest to being done. This should include all immediate concerns, whether they are writing-related or not. I'm not talking about stuff that takes five minutes, like taking out the garbage or brushing your teeth; this list is for time-consuming tasks. Not that the little stuff doesn't add up, but it is also generally stuff that can be sandwiched between other tasks.

Once you have your list, you have a better idea of tasks that need managing. Now, this list's purpose isn't to go from top to bottom — unless, of course, there is a rather urgent deadline. Mostly this list serves three purposes: to help you remember your goals and responsibilities, to put things into perspective, and to give you the satisfaction of having something to cross off as you accomplish it.

Now… take a deep breath.

Enforcing Order

The list is only the first step. Next, there are several different things you can do. If you are the type that works better with a schedule, make a schedule based on the prioritized list. If this isn't for you, though, you can set goals. Here is a list. Either borrow from it or use it to get your own ideas:

- I will complete one thing on my list a day
- If I finish a story, I can read a book for fun (or insert some other guilty pleasure)
- If I meet my deadline, my honey and I are going to dinner
- I will write XXX words today
- Between 5pm and 6pm (or whatever time best fits your schedule), I will do nothing but write
- I want to be published by the end of the year
- I will submit one story a month to a major publication
- I will sit down to write once a day

By structuring things in some way, you can exert control and keep things manageable. This doesn't mean if you can't keep that schedule or meet those goals, you do nothing; these are just things to aim for to keep you focused. Often, we feel overwhelmed because we can't get a clear picture of what needs to be done or what is most important or time-sensitive.

Discipline

When you have the time set aside to write, make sure you are writing. Don't fuss with email or chat on the phone or even think of starting up that computer game. Your time is, most likely, limited. If not, you are much more fortunate than the majority of the writers out there. Assuming you are in the limited camp, you have to put your best effort into the writing time you do have. If you aren't inspired, edit; if there is nothing to edit, research; if there is nothing to research, plan. Deviate from this too often, and you will find you have squandered the time you might have been writing. The occasional defection is to be expected; desertion is not.

Saying NO

There are times when no amount of organization or schedules or goals will do you a bit of good. Why, you ask? Because we are overachievers. We take on too much. We bury ourselves in tasks and obligations because they interest us, or because we feel (or are) obligated, or because we just don't know how to say no.

Learn. *Now.*

You can't do justice to yourself or your writing if you take on too much responsibility. This doesn't mean you have to avoid everything or that you should shirk things you truly ought to do (feeding the dog is mandatory), but you can regulate when you add new projects to your list, either of your own creation or someone else's request. For example, I am, first and foremost, a writer. However, particularly in recent years, I have also delved into being an anthology editor, a promotions manager, and a freelance typesetter. (Yeah... that masochism I mentioned earlier.) I'm sure you can imagine exactly how often those responsibilities conflict with one another. Needless to say, I have not been getting as much writing done as I might have. Clearly, I need to remember how to say No to myself. Fortunately, I can choose the projects I work on, and none of them have hard deadlines, other than the actual writing.

- If you want to be published in a major magazine, stop submitting your work to semi-pro publications,

- If you want to publish a novel, stop writing short stories for a while,

- If you have a book with a deadline, shelve the other ideas you get until you are done.

- Don't let others pressure you into taking on more projects

Letting Go

No. You can't do it all. Yes, you read me right. Sometimes you have to let projects go, at least temporarily, if not for all time. See, when you are a writer, you tend to find ideas in everything:

conversations, encounters on the street, things you see in life. I repeat: You can't do them all. There just isn't enough time. Write passing ideas down but limit yourself in how many you develop at one time. Yes, it means you might lose the thread of inspiration you first saw in it, but you are more likely to get more work completed on established projects, which means more finished projects in the end. Don't let your focus become divided. This is important because if you are going at this with an eye on a dedicated hobby (or career if you prefer), you will have to weigh what is likely to aid you to that end and attribute importance accordingly.

Summing Up

I know what it is like to want to do everything at once, and I have been in that place where I can't bring myself to do one single thing. Temper your enthusiasm, or you will burn yourself out or leave more loose threads trailing behind you than you do finished works. Do not neglect your non-writing obligations because those are the things of life, but make time for your craft because that is the essence of the soul. It is important to find a balance. Perhaps what I have written here will help you toward that end — I certainly hope so, anyway — or perhaps it will inspire you to ideas of your own. Do something, though, because this should be a joy, not a chore or a strain or a looming black cloud.

About the Author

Award-winning author, editor, and publisher Danielle Ackley-McPhail has worked both sides of the publishing industry for longer than she cares to admit. In 2014 she joined forces with husband Mike McPhail and friend Greg Schauer to form her own publishing house, eSpec Books (www.especbooks.com).

Her published works include six novels, *Yesterday's Dreams, Tomorrow's Memories, Today's Promise, The Halfling's Court, The Redcaps' Queen*, and *Baba Ali and the Clockwork Djinn*, written with Day Al-Mohamed. She is also the author of the solo collections *Eternal Wanderings, A Legacy of Stars, Consigned to the Sea, Flash in the Can, Transcendence, Between Darkness and Light*, and the non-fiction writers' guides *The Literary Handyman* and *LH: Build-A-Book Workshop*. She is the senior editor of the *Bad-Ass Faeries* anthology series, *Gaslight & Grimm, Side of Good/Side of Evil, After Punk*, and *Footprints in the Stars*. Her short stories are included in numerous other anthologies and collections.

In addition to her literary acclaim, she crafts and sells original costume horns under the moniker The Hornie Lady Custom Costume Horns, and homemade flavor-infused candied ginger under the brand of Ginger KICK! at literary conventions, on commission, and wholesale.

Danielle lives in New Jersey with husband and fellow writer, Mike McPhail and two extremely spoiled cats.

To learn more about her work, visit www.sidhenadaire.com or www.especbooks.com.

The Handyman's Helpers

Anders Håkon Gaut
Anonymous Reader
Aysha Rehm
C.J. Frost
Cato Vandrare
Cheri Kannarr
Christopher J. Burke
Christopher Weuve
Chuck Robinson
Deanna Stanley
eSpec Books
Gary Phillips
Gav
Heather Stephens
Ian Harvey
James Gotaas
Jaq Greenspon
Jen Kappert
Jennifer L. Pierce
Judi Fleming
Judith Waidlich
Kelly Pierce
L.E. Custodio
Lark Cunningham
Lorraine J. Anderson
maileguy
mdtommyd
Mike M.
Peter Engebos
pjk
Scott Schaper
Steph Parker
Stephen Ballentine
The Creative Fund
Tina M Noe Good

CPSIA information can be obtained
at www.ICGtesting.com
Printed in the USA
LVHW020950140121
676459LV00004B/219